# CLEVELAND

WHERE THE EAST COAST MEETS THE MIDWEST

BY PETER JEDICK

First Printing, 1980

Second Printing, 1993

All stories except League Park and Glenn Curtiss' Record
Flight originally appeared in *Cleveland Magazine*.

Cover design by Denise Ziganti
Design layout by Heidi Hill

Cover photo of Cuyahoga River Flats by Louie E. Anderson

Printed at Fine Line Litho Inc.
Cleveland, Ohio

ISBN 0-9605508-2-8

# Dedicated to Annie, Elsa and Rocky Jedick

# TABLE OF CONTENTS

*Cleveland as seen from the west banks of the Cuyahoga River (Ohio City) circa 1851.*

# FOREWORD

Finding reasons to be proud of Cleveland falls into and out of vogue, but for Peter Jedick it's a constant, fruitful and rewarding search. For several years, Jedick has written historical articles highlighting achievements of Cleveland and its native sons. This book is a collection of some of his best published works.

The book takes the reader on an intriguing trip down "Millionaire's Row" on Euclid Avenue then up to the cockpit that Jimmy Doolittle parachuted from here in 1929. The journey starts at a hamlet with 57 brave settlers and stops for a look at a road map through the 80s.

The trip includes a look at the construction of the Terminal Tower when an awe-struck public thought it really was the "greatest thing since the pyramids." Don't miss the tour guide's account in 1936 when Cleveland went Hollywood and held its famous air races in Los Angeles. Jedick tells you a little bit of everything. He gives accounts of the era when every fashion conscious man groomed a long handlebar moustache. He reports on Cleveland's "Black Edison" who invented the gas mask, automatic traffic signal and even a hair straightener.

This collection colorfully follows Jedick's first book, "League Park." A former Cleveland West Tech High School and Kent State University baseball player, Jedick just keeps pitching for Cleveland.

Brian Hyps
Sun Newspapers

# I.
# CLEVELAND: THE MAKING OF A CITY

## The gem of the west, the forest city, the best location in the nation...

The last time a mile-high sheet of ice visited Cleveland it rounded off the hills, filled the existing lakes and river valleys with glacial debris and created a new system of rivers and lakes. Geographers would call this new system the Great Lakes basin. The glacier that created it receded about 10,000 years ago and, as the climate warmed, animals, birds and fish entered the new forests, lakes and streams.

The first men to arrive in the territory were migrating Indian tribes. They harvested the rich hunting grounds but left few traces behind. These tribes gave way to the British and French, who began settling the New World in the 17th century and claimed the land for themselves. England's victory in the French and Indian War, which ended with the signing of the Treaty of Paris in 1763, greatly strengthened her holdings. However, in the next decade British claims were lost forever as the Americans won their independence.

The vast virgin wilderness quickly became a problem for the young nation. Different colonies claimed the region on the basis of overlaping charters, a conflict which was resolved by the Northwest Ordinance of 1787. The ordinance provided a method for allowing the disputed regions to become states, setting the pattern for future western expansion. Connecticut, in deference to its small size, was allowed to retain a portion of land bordering Lake Erie. This "Western Reserve," as it was called, was immediately put up for sale to raise money for Connecticut's public school system.

Forty-nine shareholders of the Connecticut Land Company purchased three million acres of the Western Reserve, sight unseen, for $1,200,000. In 1796 Moses Cleveland, a member of the company's board of directors, set out with a party of men to make peace with the Indians and survey the land so it could be resold and settled. The cooperation of the Indians was essential for, after General "Mad" Anthony Wayne defeated Ohio Indian tribes in 1795, the Treaty of Greenville established the Cuyahoga River as the western boundary of the United States.

Cleveland, a short, thick-set Yale graduate, lawyer, Revolutionary War captain and state representative,

*Auguste Rodin's* The Thinker *graces the entrance to the Cleveland Art Museum in University Circle.*

*Rolf Stoll's oil portrait of General Moses Cleaveland hangs in the Western Reserve Historical Society Museum.*

*The Cleveland Grays marching in the Northwest Quadrant of Public Square circa 1839.*

looked so much like an Indian that his men called him *Paqua*, after an Indian Chief. He led his party through the Hudson and Mohawk Valleys and along the shores of Lakes Ontario and Erie. At Buffalo peace was made with the Six Nation Indian tribes, who consented to allow settlement east of the Western Reserve's Cuyahoga River in exchange for 500 pounds of New York currency, two beef cattle and 100 gallons of whiskey. On July 22, 1796, Cleaveland reached the mouth of the Cuyahoga where, true to his agreement with the Indians, he landed on the river's east bank. There he began to divide into resaleable lots the tree-covered flatlands, which his men insisted he name after himself rather than the river Cuyahoga, an Indian word for "crooked."

Two men in Cleaveland's party, Amos Spafford and Seth Pease, drew plans for the new settlement in typical Connecticut small-town fashion: an open-area commons (Public Square) in the center, surrounded by 220 two-acre blocks set along rectangular streets. Despite great hardship the difficult task was completed by the end of the summer. Cleaveland returned home, never to visit his namesake again.

The following year Lorenzo Carter arrived from Vermont with his family. The Carters built a large log cabin near the mouth of the Cuyahoga, becoming the region's first permanent white settlers. While other new arrivals moved toward the nearby eastern ridges (foothills of the Appalachian mountains) to escape the disease-ridden swampland, Carter used his log cabin as a trading post, ballroom, post office, school and church. He built the first ferry to cross the Cuyahoga, supervised construction of a warehouse, settled Indian disputes and conducted the hanging of John O'Mic, an Indian convicted of killing two white trappers.

O'Mic's hanging on Public Square and the subsequent digging up of his body by some physicians was one of the main reasons the Indians on the west side of the river (the beginning of the Great Plains) joined forces with the British in the War of 1812. Few returned after the war. The west side, taking the name Ohio City, opened for settlement. On the opposite bank of the river, Cleveland, having shed the first "a" of its founder's name, officially incorporated as a village in 1815.

The village was so small that of the 12 voters who participated in its first election, nine were elected to office. Alfred Kelly, the first village president, went to the Ohio capitol as the state's youngest legislator during the period in which New York opened the Erie Canal, connecting its major city with Lake Erie. Ohio wanted to do the same thing and Kelley, serving on the state canal commission, won for Cleveland the choice spot as the northern terminus of the Ohio Canal. Kelley personally supervised construction of the canal by living along the line with the Irish and German immigrants who were

5

*Nineteenth century ore boats docked along the Cuyahoga River.*

working off their passage to America by digging the 24-foot-wide, four-foot-deep ditch. The first section opened in 1827. Soon smooth-riding "packets," each pulled by a team of three single-file horses with a boy driver, were competing with the stagecoaches and covered wagons for passengers and freight.

The canal opened the rich Ohio farmlands to eastern markets via Lake Erie and the Erie Canal, making Cleveland the frontier's marketplace. The "Gem of the West" grew 30 times its 1820 population in three decades. A shipbuilding industry thrived on the banks of the Cuyahoga and side-wheeling steamships and full-masted schooners dotted the harbor.

By 1850 the canal was diminishing in importance because of the speedy, efficient "iron horse." As early as 1836 the state granted a charter to the Cleveland, Columbus and Cincinnati railroad, but a national financial panic delayed progress until 1847 when enterprising Alfred Kelley came to the rescue. He began construction to keep the charter alive even though the company could afford only one lone worker inching toward Columbus with a wheelbarrow and shovel through the fall and winter months. In 1851 the wood-fired, brass-trimmed locomotive *Cleveland,* built at Ohio City's Steam Furnace Company, made its initial run from Columbus to Cleveland along rails imported from England.

Cleveland became an important railroad hub, no longer relying on canal transportation. Ohio City forgot its differences with its larger neighbor, even

the armed battle which had erupted over a bridge across the Cuyahoga in 1821, and the two merged in 1854.

At this time it became no longer necessary to import iron from abroad. Cleveland chemist Dr. J. Lang Cassels discovered one of the world's largest iron ore deposits while searching for copper in upper Michigan. He interested prominent businessmen in organizing the Cleveland Iron Mining Company. With the opening of the Soo Canal in 1855, acres of iron ore traveled the Great Lakes from Michigan and Minnesota to meet tons of coal from the fields of Pennsylvania, Ohio and West Virginia in "the Flats" of the Cuyahoga River valley just in time to provide the railroads and cannons needed by the Union Army in its desperate struggle with the Confederacy. During the Civil War Cleveland's economy boomed. New industrial and manufacturing plants proliferated as offshoots of the metal industry, and the working population swelled.

By 1860 almost half the city's 43,417 people were foreign-born, many of the them having immigrated from England, Scotland and Wales. The poulation doubled during each of the next two decades as Catholics, Protestants and Jews from central and eastern Europe transformed Cleveland into a "little Europe." Foreign-language newspapers multiplied, and many immigrants on their way west were attracted instead to the prosperity of Cleveland. The combination of economic opportunity and cultural mix ushered in an age of innovation and invention.

FOREST CITY HOUSE

SUPERIOR STREET, WEST FROM PUBLIC SQUARE.

*Public Square circa 1874.*

*The Spirit of '76 was painted by Cleveland artist Archibald Willard in his downtown studio for the nation's centennial celebration in 1876. This version of the famous painting is on display at Cleveland's City Hall.*

*John D. Rockefeller (left), the world's richest man, and President William McKinley (center, right) sharing a back porch with Mark Hanna (on McKinley's right) and their families.*

One of the innovators was Jeptha H. Wade. A portrait painter from Michigan who had seen Samuel Morse send a message over the first telegraph line, Wade devised an insulator which made sending messages easier. His Cleveland-based telegraph construction company eventually grew into Western Union.

Another innovator was Euclid, Ohio's Charles Brush, who, using a horse treadmill, built the first practical dynamo and developed a "light that doesn't flicker," while working at the Cleveland Telegraph Supply Company. On April 29, 1879, he illuminated Public Square with twelve 2,000 candlepower arc lamps to the amazement of thousands of spectators watching through smoke-colored glass to protect their eyes. Brush developed for Cleveland the first electric street lighting system and central power station, which he soon reproduced around the world.

An inventive Scottish bicycle manufacturer named Alexander Winton built the city's first horseless carriage in his backyard in 1896. Just two years later he negotiated one of the nation's earliest auto sales. Robert Allison, a mechanical engineer from Port Carbon, Pennsylvania paid Winton $1,000 for a one-cylinder, ice-cooled vehicle that carried two passengers at 10 miles per hour. *Plain Dealer* reporter Charles B. Shanks made a special contribution while covering a Cleveland-to-New York trip with Winton: He coined and popularized the term "automobile" which quickly supplanted the previously used "go-along" or "motor-wagon."

The automobile's consumption of fuel helped make John D. Rockefeller's fortune. Graduating from E. C. Folsom's Commercial College, Rocke-

feller had trouble finding a job. Finally hired as a bookkeeper by Hewitt and Tuttle's commission merchant house in the Flats, he became aware of the glut of oil refineries crowding the banks of the Cuyahoga and decided to find a place in the budding oil industry. With the help of Samuel Andrews, a Cleveland chemist, Rockefeller eventually monopolized the oil industry's production and distribution processes. He became the world's richest man and Cleveland became its oil refining capital. His tactics brought an onslaught of federal antitrust laws and, after a run-in with local tax officials, Rockefeller left Cleveland and his Forest Hills summer mansion. Yet following his death in 1937 at age 97, Rockefeller was buried in his home city's Lake View Cemetery.

One of Rockefeller's Central High School classmates, Mark Hanna, married into a coal and iron company where he did so well that it later became the Hanna company. Turning his energies and wealth to politics, Hanna became Ohio's Republican Party boss. Masterminding William McKinley's Presidential campaign against William Jennings Bryan in 1896, Hanna organized the most lavish propaganda machine in American politics. He blitzed the public with an advertising campaign that set the style for 20th century Presidential politicking. His efforts were rewarded with an appointment to the U.S. Senate by the Ohio legislature. But another Clevelander, anarchist Leon Czogosz, dealt a mortal blow to Hanna's power by assassinating President McKinley right after his reelection in 1901.

That same year Hanna suffered a stinging defeat in local politics. His arch rival, Tom L. Johnson, was

*Mayor Tom L. Johnson (center); Peter Witt, city clerk; Newton D. Baker, city solicitor; the embodiment of America's Progressive era.*

*East Tech High and Ohio State's Jesse Owens with his Cleveland coach and mentor, Charles Riley, before a 1935 exhibition race in Lakewood. Owens went on to win four gold medals in the 1936 Berlin Olympics.*

elected Mayor of Cleveland. Johnson had acquired a streetcar empire in Indianapolis, beginning with $30,000 he had earned at the age of 17 with the invention of a glass fare box. When he came to "The Forest City" to expand his holdings, Johnson immediately clashed with Hanna's railway company. A disciple of social reformer Henry George's single tax theory, Johnson withdrew from business and turned to a public career. As a mayor who was a "traitor to his class," he waged war against privilege. In Johnson's four terms as mayor, his administration became the embodiment of America's progressive era. Lincoln Steffens, famous muckraker and enemy of political graft, called Johnson "the best mayor of the best governed city in the United States."

Johnson's city solicitor, Newton D. Baker, later became mayor and then was appointed Secretary of War by President Woodrow Wilson. World War I brought another industrial surge, only this time the momentum continued after the fighting stopped. In the period from the 1915 opening of the Cleveland Play House to the 1931 opening of Severence Hall, most of Cleveland's enduring institutions were born: Playhouse Square on Euclid Avenue, the Metropolitan Park system, the 80,000-seat Cleveland Stadium, Wade Park and many of its cultural centers and the downtown Mall — all of which continue to leave a deep impression on the face of the city.

But it was the Van Sweringen brothers, Oris Paxton and Mantis James, who dominated the

Cleveland scene during the 1920s, much the way their Terminal Tower still dominates the Cleveland skyline. The two Wooster, Ohio farm boys turned an abandoned religious colony into the splendidly planned suburb of Shaker Heights. To promote this real estate venture they brought a transit line to the city and built a train station for its commuters. Their Terminal Tower complex, consisting of a department store, office building, bank, hotel, medical building and restaurant space for 10,000 — all within walking distance of the train station — was considered one of the most important commercial complexes in the country. And, soaring 708 feet, the 52-story Terminal Tower was the largest building in the world outside of New York City until 1967.

In 1929 the stock market crashed, the Van Sweringen's empire crumbled and Cleveland's economy buckled. The Depression forced the city to seek new solutions to old problems. Councilman Ernie Bohn began a one-man campaign to eradicate Cleveland's slums. In 1933 he wrote and pushed through the state legislature Ohio's model public housing law which created a new type of government agency, the Cleveland Metropolitan Housing Authority. Bohn convinced the federal government, under the Public Works Administration, to construct the nation's first public housing projects, the Cedar Avenue and Lakeview Terrace apartments, where slums had festered.

A less positive result of the Depression's hard

*The creators of Superman (left to right) artist Joe Shuster, Joannie Siegel (the original model for Lois Lane) and her husband, writer Jerry Siegel at home today in California. Joe and Jerry created the popular Superman comic while students at Glenville High in the early 1930's. Above, the cover from the first Superman comic book, Action Comics, June, 1938.*

times was a rise in racketeering. One of newly elected Mayor Harold Burton's first acts in 1935 was to appoint Eliot Ness as the youngest safety director in the city's history. Ness wasted no time attacking the "Cleveland Gang" and the criminals it supported. He painted the police cars red, white and blue to make the public more aware of them, busted the notorious Harvard Club casino in Newburgh Heights and investigated his own department, indicting nine police officials and forcing the resignations of many others. Mayor Burton went on to become a U.S. Senator and Supreme Court Justice.

World War II took Cleveland, like the rest of the country, out of the Depression. Postwar prosperity followed. Although Cleveland had relinquished its place as the auto manufacturing center of the nation to Detroit, it remained a major auto parts supplier. Because of new peacetime consumer demands, manufacturing plants prospered and attracted a new influx of labor. Southern blacks, Appalachian whites and Puerto Ricans joined Cleveland's already diverse ethnic population.

In the 1950's Cleveland's booming industries and championship sports teams caused it to adopt a local utility company's ad campaign slogan for its own: "The Best Location in the Nation." The opening of the St. Lawrence Seaway made Cleveland an international port. Local industrialist Cyrus Eaton cultivated "detente" with the Soviet Union despite national outrage. And Alan Freed's Moon Dog Ball at the old Cleveland Arena turned a generation onto rock 'n' roll.

The turbulent '60s were a different matter. Rising racial tensions erupted in the Hough riots of 1966. Although they represented only one link in the chain of emotional explosions against injustice across the country, the riots were uncharacteristic of a city that prided itself on race relations. Joseph Hodge, a black scout, had helped guide Moses Cleaveland to the Western Reserve, an area that later became a last gateway to freedom for escaping slaves traveling the underground railroad to Canada. In 1890 state senator John P. Green, the city's first black public official, sponsored Ohio's Labor Day holiday, four years before it became a national holiday. Cleveland Browns fullback Marion Motley and Indians outfielder Larry Doby broke down racial barriers in the sports world. So perhaps it wasn't surprising when, a year after the Hough riots, Carl Stokes (the great-grandson of a slave) defeated Seth Taft (the great-grandson of a president) to become the first black mayor of a major American city.

The new mayor inherited a city burdened by problems endemic to America's urban centers. One of the most serious—the ecological crisis—came dramatically to light when after over 100 years of supporting America's affluence, the Cuyahoga River set itself ablaze on June 22, 1969.

That and other events shocked local leaders into recognizing how devastating neglect of the city's downtown core could be. Attention began to focus on the rejuvenation of downtown Cleveland. The Cleveland Area Arts Council sponsored a series of outdoor murals, changing the drab exterior walls of various buildings into colorful works of art. Park Centre, a 1,000-suite apartment complex atop a large shopping mall, became a cornerstone of downtown redevelopment by drawing people back to the center of the city. Across from Park Centre, Chester Commons added a splash of parkland greenery for public enjoyment.

But it wasn't until Republican George Voinovich defeated Democratic Mayor Dennis Kucinich that Cleveland's true Renaissance began. Kucinich, the city's youngest mayor ever, gained popularity attacking big businesses. However, his naive style led the city into financial default.

Voinovich, on the other hand, vowed to cooperate with local businesses in streamlining government and improving Cleveland's poor national image. During his ten year reign (1979-89) Cleveland became known as the Comeback City, winning the coveted All-American City award three times. Before leaving to become Governor of Ohio, Voinovich began many of the programs that Mayor Michael White (1989-?) has nurtured to fulfillment.

In the 1980's Cleveland won a national bidding war to host the Rock and Roll Hall of Fame and Museum. The Flats entertainment district on the banks of the once maligned Cuyahoga River became one of the hottest nightlife meccas in the Midwest.

The Ohio, State and Palace theatres in Playhouse Square were saved from the wrecking ball and restored to their former glory. The Tower City complex was completed in the bowels of the Terminal Tower, combining a suburban-style shopping mall with the downtown hub of the city's transit system.

While many cities saw their sports teams flee for suburban locations, Cleveland's Gateway complex brought a new stadium and arena within walking distance of Tower City.

The Warehouse District between the Flats and Public Square renovated loft offices and apartments for a new breed of urban dweller.

Even the Metroparks Zoo jumped on the bandwagon, capping a $60 million expansion program with a $30 million RainForest exhibit.

Yet the real excitement in town is still on the horizon. After over 100 years of neglect the downtown lakefront will feature a stunning North Coast Harbor complex matching any city in the world. The Rock and Roll Hall of Fame, a Great Lakes Museum of Science, Environment and Technology and the Great Waters Aquarium will create tourist excitement not seen in Cleveland since the Great Lakes Exposition of 1936-7.

Cleveland is a city with a rich history and a vast reservoir of diverse ethnic talents. Its citizens have come together in the past two decades to create a model for other cities to copy. As it approaches its Bicentennial celebration in 1996, Cleveland is poised to take its place again as one of the great urban centers of our nation.

*Above: The Cleveland Indians new natural grass, baseball-only stadium was built in the tradition of old League Park. It has a seating capacity of 42,000. Below: The new 21,000 seat downtown arena is located in the same Gateway complex. It will host the Cleveland Cavaliers basketball team and Lumberjacks hockey team.*

14

*Above: The Cleveland Metroparks Zoo's $30 million RainForest Exhibit opened in November, 1992. It is part of an aggressive restoration of the zoo's facilities that promises even more dramatic changes in the 21st century. Below: The Tower City Complex added three levels of shops and restaurants to a newly remodeled transit station under the Terminal Tower. It also included two new office buildings and a Ritz Carlton Hotel.*

# II.
# WHEN EUCLID AVENUE WAS SOMEBODY
## "The most beautiful street in the world"

Dwelle Butts, Cleveland's bus-driving ego booster, swings his green Cleveland tours coach onto Euclid Avenue for the final leg of his two-and-a-half-hour trip. He beeps wildly to draw my attention and pulls out of the flow of traffic coming off Liberty Boulevard to pick me up. I'd been waiting to hitch a ride down what was once known as the most beautiful street in the world, Euclid Avenue, to see what traces of that age still remain.

I take the seat directly behind our host. Behind me are two elderly black ladies, both native Clevelanders rediscovering their city. Across the aisle is a middle-aged couple from New York and their teen-age daughter.

The intrusion over, Butts quickly slips back into his rat-a-tat documentary. His first comment on the once grand boulevard is about Winston Willis, the black entrepreneur who has developed the East 105th-Euclid area into a thriving entertainment center, and his second is about Bob Hope, who sold newspapers on the same corner the first time the area was a thriving entertainment center 50 years ago. Butts casually mentions that the area was once known as Doan's Corners. It was named after Job Doan, who owned most of the surrounding land long before either Winston Willis or Bob Hope arrived on the scene. Doan built a tavern on Euclid Avenue when it was still an Indian path that followed Lake Erie's old shoreline all the way to Buffalo.

Then, in 1815, Buffalo Road was renamed Euclid Avenue within the city limits. Why? Because it was the main thoroughfare to the outlying township of Euclid.

Ten years after the name change, new settlers were still clearing the land but they left enough trees so that the village would become known as "The Forest City." A new arrival sailing into the mouth of the Cuyahoga would have trouble believing anyone lived nearby. A few church spires were his only clues. But in the 1920s something happened that would change forever the destiny of the small settlement of farmers and tradesmen along the banks of a crooked little river. Cleveland was chosen as the northern terminus of the Ohio Canal and quickly became a center of trade and industry. Within years the once marshy flats of the Cuyahoga Valley became a dense

*Euclid Avenue looking west from Muirson Street (East 12th) circa 1870.*

*Sam Williamson built Euclid Avenue's first house on the corner of Public Square.*

mass of iron mills and lumberyards. The Civil War gave industry its great impetus, and for the first time in the country's history there was an opportunity for many to amass great wealth. And Cleveland, at the crossroads of the industrial revolution, was the place to make it. Along with great wealth came a tremendous purchasing power and Cleveland's instant millionaires turned their new-found riches in one direction, Euclid Avenue.

Butts knows his route and teases his riders with an offhand remark. "We're now approaching what was once Millionaires' Row. Every now and then you'll see the remains of an old mansion." Then, almost as the word mansion slips past his lips, the University Club, Anson Stager's old mansion, appears out of nowhere. It's set far enough back from the road that if you weren't looking for it you wouldn't notice it.

Millionaires' Row, just like the rest of the city, grew in bits and pieces. Sam Williamson started it off. He arrived in Cleveland in 1810 and built the city's first tannery near his home by the Cuyahoga River. A few years later, looking for more room for his growing family, he built a new home at Euclid Avenue and Public Square. Little did he

realize the trend he was setting. Sam Williamson lived to see Cleveland grow from a hamlet of 57 persons to a city of 200,000.

Other residents followed his lead as the population swelled in a southeasterly direction. But the first step in converting the simple country road into a classic boulevard was taken by Truman P. Handy, better known as "the first banker of Cleveland." Handy was *the* cashier of the Commercial Bank of Lake Erie, Cleveland's first bank, organized in 1816.

By 1842, after his bank had failed once and then reopened, he had become successful and was ready to build a new home. He chose a lot on Euclid at about East 19th Street but his old neighbors tried to talk him out of moving so far away from his place of business. Despite their objections, he built what was then considered the finest residence in Cleveland. And , as a prominent civic leader, he encouraged other notables to build "out in the country" even though Euclid was still a cinder road and the Erie (East 9th) Street intersection was so muddy and rutted from stagecoach wheels it was called "the frog pond."

Handy's friends followed his advice. Family after family of the city's emerging aristocracy chose

Euclid Avenue for their homes. It became the "in" place to live. A stranger wanting to know who the most powerful men in Cleveland were in the last half of the nineteenth century had merely to stroll down Euclid and ask who lived where.

The three decades after the Civil War were both Cleveland's and Euclid Avenue's golden era. The hardships of the pioneer days had been left behind while the evils of the machine age still lurked over the horizon. It was a time, according to Ella Grant Wilson's *Famous Old Euclid Avenue,* "when horse cars rattled over cobblestone streets, when women's skirts trailed in the dust and when downtown was west of Public Square." And "almost every man wore whiskers and a rubber collar. Bustles, balloon sleeves and funny hats were in vogue for women. The tallest building in town was six stories, saloons and grog shops almost rubbed elbows, and horses, hitched tandem, pranced down Euclid Avenue in the shade of stately elms."

It was the stately elms, and the residences beneath them, that made Euclid Avenue world-famous. In 1860 John Fiske, a popular writer, described the avenue in a lecture before the Royal Society of Great Britain: "Bordered on each side with a double row of arching trees, and with handsome stone houses of sufficient variety and freedom of arhitechtural design, standing at intervals of one to two hundred feet along the entire length of the street . . . the vistas reminding one of the nave and aisles of a huge cathedral."

It was a liberal sprinkling of the majestic elms plus an ornate landscaping of the huge grounds between the homes which made Euclid Avenue unique. It seemed more like a park than a street.

While America's *nouveau riche* were building brownstone fronts along New York's Fifth Avenue and other such streets, Cleveland's newly-rich were pioneering the suburban concept. The eastern cities were borrowing their building ideas from London (city folks) while Cleveland was being true to its heritage (country folks). And, as country folks might do, it wasn't uncommon to find the family cow grazing along the avenue's spacious front lawns.

Warren Wick remembers one such cow interfering with his boyhood plans to build a tennis court at the corner of Sterling (East 30th) and Euclid. Wick, a retired investment banker, grew up in a yellow-and-white house where the United Way building now stands at 3100 Euclid. The cow was owned by his next-door neighbor, William A. Leonard, Episcopal bishop of Ohio. He grazed the cow in the empty lot where Warren and his friend, Elton Hoyt, envisioned a lawn tennis court. In the spirit of the times Bishop Leonard shortened the cow's towline so the boys could mark off their court in the far corner of the property.

Wick's older brother, Dudley, was a budding scientist and used their home as a testing ground for his experiments. While electricity was still a virtually unknown phenomenon, he installed a burglar alarm system, electric starters for the gas lighters and his own dynamo. While attending Central High School, he assisted Dr. Dayton Miller of old Case School of Applied Science in developing the first X-ray machine in the U.S. Dudley took the country's first X-ray, a shot of his own left hand, on February 14, 1896. He died tragically nine years later from overexposure to the rays.

Both Warren Wick and Revely G. Beattie, another native of that era, remember Euclid's being portrayed as "the most beautiful street in the world" in their schoolbooks. This tribute, eagerly repeated by the city's natives, was given the avenue by Bayard Taylor, an American traveler and author who visited Cleveland frequently. He stated that only the Prospekt Nevsky in St. Petersburg (today Leningrad) matched its beauty. Others compared it with the Champs Elysees in Paris and the Unter den Linden in Berlin. It was claimed that "no other avenue in the world presented such a continous succession of charming residences and such uniformly beautiful grounds for so great a distance."

If a Clevelander was visiting another city the first reaction he invariable received was, "Ah, Euclid Avenue." Its fame was such that a butler, Samuel Milliken, once received a letter from Europe addressed simply, "Samuel Milliken, Euclid Avenue." There was no need to add anything further.

Such bouquets hardly could go unnoticed. Euclid Avenue became more than a civic asset; it was a spiritual reservoir, the American dream stretched out along a cobblestone boulevard for all the world to sit back and pay homage. Its grandeur testified to the 19th-century business philosophy of Social Darwinism, the application of Darwin's famous "survival of the fittest" evolution formula to social organization. The new ruling class, the industrialist and the investment banker who made their fortunes in the industrial revolution, believed they got where they were because they deserved it and those who didn't, didn't. "God gave me my money," explained John D. Rockefeller. And Rockefeller was only one of Cleveland's wealthy who owned a home on Euclid Avenue.

That these homes were built to last forever was never questioned. They were to be used as centers of great social and political gatherings since, by the era of Reconstruction, Euclid Avenue's residents were exerting tremendous power not only on the local scene, but at the national level.

Daniel P. Eells made his fortune developing railroads. In 1881 the library of his Euclid Avenue estate was the scene of a conference between himself, Marcus Hanna (another Euclid Avenue resident) and William McKinley.

Hanna was looking for a politician like McKinley to take under his wing. With Hanna's backing McKinley became the Governor of Ohio and then the President of the United States.

On the corner of Euclid and North Perry (East 21st) stood Senator Henry Payne's massive stone house. In his gabled residence with its stone-railed

*Progressive mayor Tom L. Johnson's home (above) and Andrew's Folly, a 33 room castle on the corner of Sterling (East 30th) that the Andrew's family quickly abandoned.*

*Amasa Stone's mansion (above) housed John Hay, Lincoln's secretary, until his own home was built next door. John D. Rockefeller, founder of Standard Oil and the richest man in the world, lived on the southwest corner of Case Avenue (East 40th).*

*The Anson Stager-T.S. Beckwith mansion is one of the few remaining examples of Euclid Avenue's golden era.*

portico, railroads were planned, Civil War Reconstruction organized and political strategy developed.

Up Euclid on the corner of Case (East 40th), Col. Sylvester T. Everett in 1883 built the most costly home yet. The railroad magnate-financier used his brownstone mansion to entertain Presidents Grant, Hayes, McKinley and Taft, as well as such captains of industry as Andrew Carnegie and J. Pierpont Morgan.

Across Case from Everett's, General Grant could remember picking Malaga grapes from Jeptha H. Wade's famous garden. The benefactor of Wade Park, who began his career as a portrait painter, built his fortune consolidating telegraph companies into Western Union. The seven monumental pillars used as cornerstones for his iron fence cost $1,000 apiece, a fabulous sum.

Even the backyards were unique. Charles Brush, developer of the arc light, lived where the Arena once stood. His basement laboratory was powered by an enormous backyard windmill. Tom L. Johnson, successful millionaire turned radical mayor in 1901, kept an ice skating rink in his Euclid backyard to entertain distinguished guests and neighborhood

youth. Statesmen, scientists, financiers and industrialists lined both sides of the boulevard in a wide array of architectural achievements.

But the one mansion which symbolized both Euclid Avenue's glory and tragedy was Samuel Andrews' castle. Andrews, whose process for refining crude oil provided the key to Rockefeller's Standard Oil Co. empire, took three years to build a 33-room mansion with castle-like towers and turrets. Such was his belief in the street's reputation that he had all his furnishings imported from England in anticipation of a visit from Queen Victoria. Not only did Queen Victoria fail to show, the Andrews themselves moved out within a few years. Their 33-room white elephant, complete with 100 servants, was too much for even a Standard Oil magnate to support. The empty castle was known as "Andrews' Folly" until it was replaced by a miniature golf course in 1923.

Yet Andrews' fantasies of a visit from Queen Victoria were not so farfetched for a Euclid Avenue habitue. Distinguished visitors routinely appeared here. Cleveland, on the basis of its economic strength, had moved into the forefront of national affairs. Its Euclid Avenue upstarts were influencing

*Colonel Sylvester T. Everett's music room entertained presidents and captains of industry.*

seats of power formerly held by southern planters and northern merchants, the old aristocracy of inherited wealth.

Obviously the old aristocracy didn't take a particularly sympathetic view to the newcomers. John Hay's novel, *The Breadwinners,* illustrates this view. Hay, secretary to President Lincoln and later secretary of state under McKinley, spent five years in Cleveland after marrying the wealthy Amasa Stone's daughter, Clara. Stone wanted his daughter near him while he was ill and also wanted Hay to do something more manly than write for a newspaper. (Hay was on the staff of the *New York Tribune.*) So Stone built a fashionable residence for the couple next to his own mansion on Euclid and Brownell (East 14th). At the time, Stone declared he was "building a barn for my Hay" which was exactly the kind of comment that nauseated the blue-blood diplomat. Hay wrote *The Breadwinners* during his Cleveland stay and published it anonymously as a social study. His in-depth view of the personal lives of the Euclid Avenue residents was intended as a criticism of their crassness. Instead, it revealed the resentment of the old order at being dethroned.

Of course their life style was extravagant. What was one to do with those great piles of greenbacks? The income tax and welfare state were generations away. Philanthrophy was a full-time profession.

But Ella Grant Wilson gives us an indication of the dollar's more mundane uses. As one of Cleveland's leading florists, she was welcome on Millionaires' Row. She tells of one seven-course meal for seven millionaires and their wives where the table's linen, service and floral arrangements were changed with each course. "In those days, wines were served with each course and I think the guests must have been pretty mellow by the time they had finished the famous brands set forth."

Julia Raymond in her *Recollections of Euclid Avenue* details the feminine life style in the age of Saturday baths: "I asked mother what young ladies did in the years after school before they settled down to married life. No one 'came out' in those days. Were there any committees? No. Or sewing circles? . . . As a matter of fact none of the girls could sew well except Jessie Taintor . . . The young ladies made their beds and dusted their rooms and on Saturdays cleaned the ornaments in the whatnots

*Arc light inventor Charles Brush's backyard windmill (opposite page) and Euclid Avenue mansion which included a pipe organ that stretched from the first floor up to the third story ballroom.*

that stood in every parlor. Finally, mother said, they were elevated to arranging the flowers. But, besides these, no tasks seem to have been expected of them." She recalled her mother once receiving a diamond ring for baking a loaf of bread.

Despite the great material gulf separating the Euclid residents from the rest of Cleveland, there was one ritual that all Clevelanders shared in, and it added immensely to the street's reputation: the Euclid Avenue sleigh races, a six-week, nonstop informal winter festival.

The sleigh driver might have been a Rockefeller, a Hanna, a Bolton or an Otis, but the spirited races were open to everyone who owned a horse. There were no official starters, no timers and no judges. Applause from the crowds that lined the sidewalks was the only reward for winning. The races were purely spontaneous. A driver would move slowly eastward from Erie Street and then turn at Perry and maybe Case and line up an opponent. Heading westward the two sleighs would charge neck and neck back to Erie with the possible intention of having an exciting brush with a friend or foe who had been singled out beforehand. And while the local aristocracy dominated the scene in elegant two-horse sleighs, complete with driver, footman and charcoal foot warmer, others came from as far away as Doan's Corners.

Warren Wick remembered trying to hook his sled on the back of John D. Rockefeller's sleigh as it sped down to the Euclid Avenue Baptist Church each Sunday morning at exactly 10:10. He and his friends would try to hitch up to the sleigh only to receive a taste of the footman's whip. "It used to sting, but us kids kept trying," Wick recalled.

Today, the sleigh races, like the gaslights that kept them going through the night, long since have fallen victim to the machine age. Today's stately elm is a stark telephone pole, its branches covered with harsh electric lights, tangles of wires and voltage regulators. A major section of the street is merely a line of barred storefront windows.

Yet there are some signs that what is left of "the most beautiful street in the world" may be preserved. The University Club at 3813 Euclid was formerly Anson Stager's mansion. Stager was general superintendent of the Western Union Telegraph Company, directing the Union's telegraph lines during the Civil War. It was recently purchased by Thomas Roulston, president of the Roulston Company, who plans to spend $1.5 million to restore it as a private club.

Further down the avenue Samuel Mather's 45 room mansion still stands like a ghost house on the artificial hill created when the Innerbelt Highway cut beneath Euclid Avenue. The one time Mather estate was taken over by the Cleveland Automobile

RESIDENCE OF A. P. WINSLOW ESQ. Nº 630 EUCLID AVENUE, CLEVELAND, OHIO

*Summer and winter street scenes out of Euclid Avenue's past.*

Club in 1940 and expropriated by Cleveland State University for administrative offices in 1968.

Perhaps CSU can succeed where Samuel Mather failed. In 1907 the descendant of Puritan ministers Cotton and Increase Mather commissioned the prominent Cleveland architect Charles F. Schweinfurth (who also designed Trinity Cathedral at East 22nd) to create the most expensive home ever built in Cleveland. Mather, who made his fortune mining iron ore, hoped that such a great investment at such a late date would forestall the avenue's desertion by Cleveland's first families. But as both Dan Harbaugh, a 73-year-old retired banker who grew up near Euclid and Bolton (East 89th), and Warren Wick recalled, "the Heights" had already replaced Euclid Avenue as the place to live. New forms of architecture already were supplanting Schweinfurth's massive Romanesque style. The retreat to the suburbs had begun. The old gang was definitely breaking up, and one by one the old residences were overcome by that greatest of all evils, creeping commercialism.

Back in 1870 when Millionaires' Row was just beginning to take form, a couple Bostonians planned to open a dry goods store on the corner of Euclid Avenue and Public Square. Local commercial prophets scoffed. Everyone knew the highclass retail section of Cleveland was Superior Street. But William Taylor and Thomas Kilpatrick pinned their hopes on a brand-new merchandising concept, "the one-price system."

They publicized their new idea in the *Cleveland Herald* on the day of their grand opening. "Our goods are bought in the present low market and will be sold exclusively at the one-price system at popular prices." This meant the same price would be given each customer on the same piece of goods. Prior to the Taylor-Kilpatrick policy an item's final price was the product of a bartering exchange between the customer and merchant. Their method caught on, their store was a success and Euclid Avenue's destiny was changed forever.

Slowly but surely other commercial enterprises inched up the boulevard. In 1871 Burrows' book store opened several blocks east of Public Square. In 1873 the Standard Block, home office of Standard Oil, was erected on the north side of Euclid. By 1895 Henry Chisholm's mansion between Bond (East 6th) and Erie was razed to make room for a new 14-story sandstone office building. It marked the beginning of the end of the glory that was Euclid's.

Why wasn't anything done once these evil omens began to appear? One attempt was made to preserve the avenue. On April 19, 1897, City Council passed a resolution making Euclid Avenue a boulevard and placing its care under the Board of Park Commissioners. The resolution recognized the street's worldwide reputation and stated the hope that Euclid Avenue could be maintained as a magnificent parkway connecting the center city with a new park system that one day would encircle the city.

The other main roads were to follow Euclid Avenue's example, like green spokes in the Emerald Necklace's wheel.

But too much money already had been invested in Euclid Avenue's success as a commercial enterprise. Within weeks, over 30 lawsuits were filed in Common Pleas Court contesting the constitutionality of the resolution and demanding property damages up to $100,000 if the resolution was upheld.

Three years later the park commission gave up its ill-fated task and asked the city to rescind the resolution and dismiss the court cases. The same philosophy that created the wealth to build Euclid Avenue had insured its destruction. By the 1930s John D. Rockefeller's symbol of wealth and accomplishment was razed to make room for a gas station and parking lot. A new generation of investors demanded their share of God's blessings, and in the process a proud avenue was destroyed. Most of the mansions were razed in the years after World War II to make way for cheap office buildings and warehouses.

That Euclid Avenue could have been preserved is not mere speculation. The few remaining mansions that have been converted to meet new needs offer convincing proof. Their success illustrates that the avenue's destruction was never necessary, only profitable.

After all, Euclid Avenue today is far more valuable than the Euclid Avenue of the past. Land once sold for 20 cents an acre is today worth more than $50 a square foot. But certain things once lost are impossible to ever regain. At one time the first place a Clevelander took a visitor was for a ride down Euclid Avenue. Today an out-of-state license plate on the same street is a rarity.

As early as 1918 Ihna T. Frary, a native Clevelander and architectural historian, lamented the great street's passing in the *Architectural Record:*

"It is too late now to redeem this lost opportunity, but it is to be hoped that the departing glory of Euclid Avenue may prove an object lesson to other communities and bring home to them the necessity for more intelligent control of municipal planning and development."

But no one listened. Forty-one years later, in a 1959 *Architectural Record* article, Richard A. Miller, an Elyria architect, called Euclid's downtown office buildings "an architectural planning fiasco."

Finally, in 1963, downtown architect Rudolph Orgler proposed a positive response to the criticism. He suggested closing the lower part of the avenue to traffic and creating an outdoor shopping mall. Mayor Ralph S. Locher turned the idea over to his experts for study. The idea is still being studied.

Even though Euclid Avenue can never hope to emulate what it once was, a beautiful outdoor shopping plaza with sidewalk cafes, art displays and street vendors would go a long way to appeasing the broken spirits of the past.

# III.
# THE TERMINAL TOWER
## They called it the greatest thing since the pyramids

O.P. and M.J. Van Sweringen stood by their Marshall Building office window surveying the scene below. They paid little attention to the dark suited men and ladies in white dresses boarding the streetcars on Public Square. They focused instead on the weird collection of dilapidated wooden structures stretching from the southwest corner of the square to the banks of the Cuyahoga River. This was by far the rankest, rowdiest, most notorious chunk of Cleveland and, if the two teetotalling brothers could only get Peter Witt off their back, they would convert it into the greatest real estate development since the Pyramids.

The year was 1919 and Cleveland was in desperate need of a railroad station large enough to handle the great volume of 20th century rail traffic. The old Union Depot, home of the Pennsylvania and New York Central railroads, had been billed as the "largest building under one roof in the United States" at its dedication in 1866. Its arched roof had been uniquely constructed so no pillars would be needed for support. But by the turn of the century the depot was a soot covered monstrosity, the butt of numerous jokes on the local vaudeville circuit and an inspiration to advertising executive Charles Bryan, who put up a billboard reading DON'T JUDGE THIS TOWN BY THIS DEPOT near its West 9th Street lakefront location. The smaller depots of the smaller railroads were in even worse condition.

Four years earlier, in 1915, Cleveland's voters had approved plans for a $16 million dollar station that would gather all the railroads into a central location at the north end of the Mall. It was to be the final touch on Mayor Tom L. Johnson's "Group" Plan. Designed by architect Daniel H. Burnham of 1893 Chicago Exposition fame, the Group Plan called for all of Cleveland's important public buildings on the square and Mall to be built the same height, of a complementary French baroque style and with an open park, the Mall in the middle offering a clear view of Lake Erie. It was the boldest example of city planning since Pierre Charles L'Enfant designed the nation's capitol in 1791, and the buildings still stand downtown today. But construction of the station was postponed by

*The Terminal Tower complex.*

M.J. VAN SWERINGEN                    O.P. VAN SWERINGEN

World War I.

In the meantime, the Van Swerigen brothers had entered the picture. The two farm boys from Wooster, Ohio had moved with their family to Cleveland's East Side at an early age. The elder by two years, Oris Paxton, or "O.P." (the brothers were always called by their initials), was short and unassuming, with a dark complexion, a slow body and a quick mind. The younger, Mantis James, or "M.J.", was the fair-haired, lighter skinned, more energetic partner. He seemed to feel his brother O.P. was his to protect and manage. If they went on a trip it was M.J. who would pack his brother's bag, buy the tickets and make reservations.

Growing up in a strict, God-fearing Dutch houshold (the boys weren't allowed to whistle on Sundays), they took on a paper route in a rural area that would one day become Shaker Heights. Their life-long business partnership had begun.

In 1896, while the boys were working together at a neighborhood grocery, their father died. O.P., who was in the eigth grade, quit school to help support the family. He became a $15-a-week clerk for the Bradley Fertilizer Company. At 21 he resigned to enter the real estate business, obtaining an option on a house on Carnegie Avenue. He sold it 24 hours later for $100 profit. He was hooked. M.J., who had followed O.P. to Bradley's, soon joined his brother in the new venture. As if playing a lifesize game of Monopoly, they began buying and selling homes in Cleveland Heights and Lakewood.

They soon became interested in a large tract of land on their old newspaper route. Just far enough away from the city to make it convenient, the land had been abandoned by the Shakers, a communal, celibate religious sect named for the ecstatic dancing that accompanied their services.

The Vans, as they were commonly known, decided to go for broke and plan a very expensive, very exclusive community with wide lawns and boulevards and a strict building code. It became Shaker Heights. In 1906 they put together over a million dollars and bought 1,366 acres of Shaker land.

J. Paul Thompson, who kept his law office open until he was 94 years old, remembered that his friend George Hale, the Shaker Heights construction chief, would build one house and then have to wait until it was sold to start another. After a few years Hale became fed up and quit. "They (the Vans) were always over their heads in debt," Thompson recalled.

Their project having bogged down, the two brothers went to New York to buy an old farm. There they struck gold in the form of Alfred H. Smith, the senior vice president of the New York Central Railroad, whose family owned the farm. Trust-busting was the current rage and Smith could read the writing on the rails. It wouldn't be too long before NYC would be forced to sell its subsidiary, the Nickel Plate, and he wanted to make sure it fell into friendly hands.

In 1915 when Attorney General Thomas Gregory instructed Smith, by then president of NYC, to dispose of the Nickel Plate under the Clayton Anti-

Trust Act, he immediately shot off a telegram to the Vans telling them that everything was set. The brothers bought the $73-million railroad for $8 million, a bargain basement price. The Vans put up $2 million—$520,000 of their own money and a million and a half borrowed from two Cleveland banks. Under a long-term easy payment plan they would pay off the rest from Nickel Plate profits.

For the Vans, buying the Nickel Plate (NKP) right-of-way cleared away the final obstacle to their ambitious plan to run a rapid transit line from downtown to their Shaker development along Kingsbury Ravine. Smith provided the Vans with invaluable counsel and financial assistance in their new enterprise, railroading, and the Vans represented the NYC's interests in Cleveland while appearing to be independent. "They went to New York to buy a farm and came back with a partner," was a popular saying at the time, according to Ernie Bohn, the father of public housing in Cleveland.

The Shaker Rapid, almost entirely financed by the NYC, provided the key link to their housing development; homes were selling as fast as they could be built. And the Nickel Plate, once denounced by Mayor Newton D. Baker as "a streak of rust, a toy railroad that runs its trains just often enough to make it dangerous," was quickly developing into one of the finest railroads in the country under the able direction of John Joseph Bernet, Smith's protege, on loan to the Vans to make sure the NKP made enough to pay off the debt.

The Vans' fortunes boomed right along with the rest of the country's. The War To End All Wars ended and America entered a decade of extreme exuberance. Cleveland, the nation's fifth largest city and growing fast, felt the need for a new train station more each day. As the old 1915 plans were being dusted off, Smith and the Vans presented their own alternative to the Group Plan: a huge station on the southwest corner of Public Square that would provide easy access to both their Shaker Rapid and NKP lines as well as to the New York Central. A lakefront station would benefit only the NYC's arch-enemy, the Pennsylvania railroad, whose tracks ran right along the Mall site. The Vans, themselves so publicity-shy they hired a newspaperman to keep their names out of the papers, launched a publicity campaign to promote their proposal.

They campaigned on two different fronts. First they promised jobs to the returning soldiers, covering the city with posters which showed the "doughboys" in battle trenches against a background depicting construction workers in civilian clothes. Second, they promised to eliminate Cleveland's major downtown eyesore—the slums surrounding Public Square.

Despite furious opposition from Peter Witt, an outspoken councilman and disciple of Tom Johnson's Group Plan who publicized the Vans' connection with the NYC, the brothers got their proposal on the ballot where it passed by a slim margin. "The Biggest Improvement in the History of Cleveland, Without a Dollar of Expense to the People" was about to begin.

The Vans quickly moved into action. Not only would they build a railroad station, but also a hotel, a department store, a bank, a medical building, enough restaurants to feed 10,000 and an office building—a veritable city within a city— all within walking distance of the train station. And the terminal itself, rather than having the small rounded dome the voters had approved, would be topped by a 52-story, 708 foot tower with a wedding cake top. It would be "the largest building in the world outside of New York City." (Paris' Eiffel Tower at 985 feet

*In 1915 Cleveland voters approved plans for this $16 million, French baroque-style railroad station to be built on the north end of the Mall. Construction was postponed by World War I.*

*As the Vans envisioned it, Cleveland's new Union Station would be a city within a city, including not only a terminal but a hotel, a bank, a department store and an office building as well.*

was taller but it wasn't considered a building.) In a complicated legal maneuver pioneered by the Cleveland Athletic Club and more recently applied in New York's Grand Central Station, the revenue from the "air rights" or office space would be used to pay off the terminal. The two parts were owned by two different companies but both were controlled by the NYC.

Today massive urban construction projects are as commonplace as the pigeons on Public Square. In 1920, however, the Terminal Tower was Cleveland's introduction to the 20th century world of Buck Rogers. It marked the beginning of the transformation of an overgrown small town into a modern metropolis. As newspapers across the country flashed the headline, CLEVELAND'S NEW UNION STATION TO BE AS LARGE AS BUILDING CODE PERMITS, the clearing of the 35-acre plot began with a vengeance. H. D. Jouett, designer of Grand Central Station, was the chief engineer of the project, designed by architects Graham, Anderson, Probst and White. It was advertised as "the greatest peace-time engineering feat since the digging of the Panama Canal." It promised to move more earth than Egypt's Great Pyramid in one-hundredth the time.

It would also move: the White Elephant, with its vaudeville song and dance teams, its jugglers and its sad comedians; Rafferty's Monkey House, with its steelworkers and lumbermen chugging nickel mugs of beer while caged simians looked on; the colony of Gypsy musicians on Hill Street; the houses of ill repute on Commercial Avenue; the restaurants on Diebolt Alley; the pawn shops with "pullerins" standing on the doorsteps; the painless dentists with their sets of false teeth smiling their gummy smiles out from little glass cases; the police station; the empty lots where vagrants slept under burlap bag tents; the tenement houses; May's 24-hour drug store that had no locks; the American, Cleveland's oldest tavern; the Forest City House, home of Cleveland's earliest theatrical adventure; the Telephone company, three cemeteries, two breweries and a fire station.

"Panama" steam shovels took one whole bank of the Cuyahoga River, put it in railroad cars and dumped it on the other side of the river beneath the Clark Avenue bridge. In all, over 1,500 buildings and three million cubic yards of material would be uprooted.

And, most amazing of all, the whole city-within-a-city would be built on quicksand.

To support the structure 87 ballshaped shafts

were dug into the bedrock 155 feet below. "Sand-hogs"—primarily Irish immigrants who, like most of the men who built the terminal, weren't Clevelanders as had been promised, but itinerant craftsmen who threw up skyscrapers at 98½ cents an hour—were lowered into the shafts by electric hoists. There they dug out the stones and dirt by hand. George Spicer of Lakewood, who at 79 years of age still cut stone for light construction projects, worked on the Terminal Tower for a year and eight months. He remembered the experience with more than a touch of bitterness.

"Slaves. They treated us like slaves," he angrily recalled in his thick Irish brogue.

Two of his companions, Patrick Toolis, 29, and Patrick Cleary, 27, were on the bottom of a 103-foot shaft when liquid cement pouring into the adjacent shaft broke through the dirt wall. The two men were covered with over 50 tons of cement. Throughout the night their fellow workers attacked the mass of concrete with air hammers, fighting off "the bends" from the subterranean gases while knowing their efforts were probably futile. At 2:35 a.m. they found the bodies, arms stretched upwards as if reaching for the cables. "It was Pud's (Cleary's) first time down," Spicer said sadly. For this dangerous work the sandhogs got $1.10 an hour.

Once the cement roots were finished and the steel skeleton bolted upward, accidents were more frequent though less spectacular. A small army of over 4,500 men worked at a breakneck pace 24 hours a day all year round. "If you couldn't keep up the pace, you were sent home the same day," said Anthony Gielty, another Irishman, who worked an electric hoist. "A lot of men only worked four hours." Walking on wet or even ice-laden steel girders, throwing hot rivets and mixing cement as they went, the laborers constantly flirted with danger.

One day a crane (they were taken apart and reassembled on each successive floor) knocked down the scaffold on which Spicer stood as he guided large tombstone-sized blocks of Bedford granite into place. He grabbed a rope and dangled there with six broken ribs and torn hands, waiting for the crane bucket to rescue him. The two other men on the scaffold fell 28 floors, bouncing off steel girders and landing in a heap of metal.

Where were the unions? "They were a joke," Spicer said. "You needed seven witnesses to file a complaint." And men were afraid to come forward "for fear of being laid off."

Finally, after about a year of continually rising compensation costs, the State of Ohio, which was footing the bill, sent a team of officials down to inspect the project. They halted construction until all the equipment was made safe. "It slowed production a bit," Spicer conceded, "but it ended the massacre."

As the tower mounted upward so did the Vans' paper empire. They began buying railroads the way children collect baseball cards, repeating again and again the magic formula that had worked so well when they bought the Nickel Plate. They would form

A construction worker poses as the flag pole on the yet to be completed terminal.

*During the height of construction workers constantly flirted with danger.*

a holding company to buy a railroad, borrow against the mother holding company to finance it, and sell enough preferred stock to the investing public to pay for it. Then they would issue a load of worthless common stock, keeping most of it themselves to retain control of the company without putting up any of their own money. In this way they gained control of the Hocking Valley Railroad, for example, while owning less than 1 percent of it.

Attracting investors was as easy as catching fish in Lake Erie. Especially when, as Nat Howard, former editor of the *Cleveland News* remembered, "The Vans were their own best cheerleaders." They became overnight sensations on Wall Street by taking advantage of the change in government policy under Calvin ("The Business of America is Business") Coolidge, who encouraged mergers as a way of bringing greater efficiency to the nation's beleaguered railroads.

Despite their rise into national prominence, the shy, sophisticated farm boys (O.P's favorite author was Rand-McNally — "because he makes the best maps") kept their home at Daisy Hill, a 65-acre estate near the Chagrin River in Hunting Valley, and concentrated on remaking the city's face. The terminal project was causing a chain reaction effect that demanded their constant attention. To replace the

old police station, which had been demolished to make way for the tower, the Vans promised to build "the finest police station in the country" on Payne Avenue. In order to provide access to the terminal for the seven associated railroads (the Pennsylvania boycotted the station), 40 steel and concrete bridges were built. To keep the smoky steam engines away from downtown, secondary stations were built at Collinwood and Linndale, at which the trains were hooked up to electric engines. When the Vans needed a department store to fill the new 12-story building flanking the tower they bought Higbee's. They even bought up a right-of-way for a new regional transit system that would connect Euclid, Parma and Rocky River to the terminal.

Finally, on August 19, 1927, "Whitey" Nelson and Louie Markberry, a couple of "connectors" (the men who connect steel beams for the riveters) raised the American flag high atop the unfinished structure. The ironworkers "doffed their hats with grimy hands," as a throng cheered 708 feet below.

The first train entered the unfinished station two years later on December 1, 1929. Many Clevelanders traveled all the way to Detroit to ride in that first train, NKP engine number 288, which, in the finest railroad tradition, arrived an hour and 40 minutes late. Over 500 spectators watched M.J. meet the train. O.P. stayed home in bed and M.J. refused to allow himself to be photographed. "They were an odd pair of fellows," recalled J. Paul Thompson.

On June 28, 1930 more than 2,500 industrial and civic leaders from all over the contry attended the dedication dinner in the chandeliered grand concourse. The NYC band played in the background while the visiting dignitaries toured the four-story-high marble floored and marble walled portico with its seven-part mural by Lincoln Memorial artist Jules Guerin. If anyone had wished to congratulate the Van Sweringens on a job well done, they must have been disappointed. The Vans failed to show up. In keeping with their image of great public modesty they listened to the dedication via a special telephone hookup to their Daisy Hill estate.

They must have felt a bit uneasy listening to NYC's president P. E. Crowley (Smith died before the terminal was completed) tell the sudience: "I believe that we have turned the corner; that we will slowly but surely go forward to at least as great prosperity as has ever been attained." The opening of the great tower was to Crowley "a symbol of our confidence in the future."

The sad fact of the matter was that the railroads, whose business has always depended on the business of the rest of the country, had been among the hardest hit by the stock market crash. And the Vans, who owned six major railroads worth over three billion dollars at the time of the crash, were broke. Their holding company empire, which was dependent on the railroads earning ever-increasing common stock dividends to pay off their debts came tumbling down. The J.P. Morgan Company, in one of Wall Street's most closely guarded secrets, rescued the Vans with a $40 million loan and a $100,000 a year expense account to enable them to keep up appearances. The Morgan firm stepped in because had the Vans gone bankrupt they would have taken the Paine Webber Company, one of America's largest brokerage firms, with them. An if Paine Webber went many of the smaller Wall Street firms

*An almost completed city landmark.*

*The ticket lobby (above), main concourse (below left) and night view of the tower during its heyday as a busy train station. The skylight above the main concourse is due to be reopened as part of a major renovation.*

would fall like dominoes. The Terminal Tower, born in the wild eyed optimism of the Twenties, reached puberty at the opening of one of America's darkest decades.

As the economy sickened and the bread lines grew longer, Cleveland's new landmark offered a ray of hope to a city wrapped in despair. From as far away as 60 miles its six giant beacons and illuminated top appeared as a new light in the evening sky. If man could construct on a patch of quicksand in 10 short years a tower tall enough to touch the sky, efficient enough to pay for itself, and large enough to combine transportation, vocation, dining and shopping under one roof, then there was no telling what he might build from the ashes of the stock market crash.

In the 1930s the Terminal Tower was the throbbing heartbeat of the city. More than 85 trains, at all hours of the day and night and from all over the country, passed through its depths. Newlyweds and movie stars, businessmen and sports heroes, immigrants and politicians, families and friends — all mingled together in the daily drama of welcomes and farewells.

Clevelanders beamed with pride over their new landmark, but began to change their opinion of the Van Sweringens, who were unable to pay their debt to the Morgan Company. When it grew to $73 million they decided to collect what they could. In September 1935 the Van Sweringens' entire holdings were put up for sale in one of Wall Street's most spectacular auctions. O.P., making one of his rare public appearances, sat quietly in the back row at the auction and bought back controlling interest in his company with $3 million borrowed from Mason jar king George Ball and Great Lakes shipping magnate George Tomlinson. "I would have rather paid the debt," the humiliated O. P. confessed to reporters afterwards.

Although the Vans were ready to try to recoup their lost empire the death of M. J. at 54 a few months later took the fight out of O. P. The two brothers had been inseparable. Never finding time away from their business to marry, they shared the same bank account and slept in twin beds until their final days. (Don't jump to any hasty conclusions. As J. Paul Thompson remembers, "they weren't drinkers but they did love the ladies" and rumors about their 36th floor suite in the terminal, the Greenbrier Room, constantly buzzed around town.) With M. J. gone O. P. lost his ambition. He spent his final years answering questions before the Senate Banking Committee on his holding company tactics. He was also indicted by a Cuyahoga County Grand Jury for allegedly selling the Union Trust Bank of Cleveland $10 million in bonds and buying them

back 10 days later to misrepresent the company's financial value. In 1936, before his case could be brought to trial, O.P. died of a heart attack in his private railroad car at the Hoboken, New Jersey yards.

He left over $61 million in debts including $14 million owed to the Union Trust Bank and four million to the local Guardian Trust. The Vans' collapse was a primary reason in both banks folding, taking with them the life savings of many Clevelanders. It would be many years before Cleveland's banks would again dare finance Van Sweringen-size projects.

No city streets were ever dedicated nor terminal plaques erected to the memory of the two brothers. Yet they had a greater impact on the city than anyone since Moses Cleaveland. A quarter-century later when CTS built a rapid transit line it used the same right-of-way the Vans had left half-built when the Depression hit. Every weekday 20,000 commuters empty from the trains into the bowels of the building that is the brothers' only monument.

Back in 1938, when the Indians' pennant fluttered from the tower's flagpole alongside Old Glory on home game dates, the "Come to Cleveland Committee" sponsored a baseball catch from the top of the Terminal Tower. As radios and newsreel cameras caught the action and 10,000 spectators swarmed over the square and peered from nearby office windows, catchers Hank Helf and Frankie Pytlak, wearing steel helmets, caught the 138-mile-per-hour balls dropped by third baseman Kenny Keltner to break Gabby Street's 1908 Washington Monument record. It was great publicity for a day.

In 1980 the newly steam-cleaned tower celebrated its 50th anniversary with a gala week long celebration, including a repeat of the 1938 stunt using a softball instead. Mike Zarefoss, an outfielder for the Cleveland Competitors pro softball team, caught the throw from Ted Stepien, the team's owner.

In 1983 Forest City Enterprises bought the Terminal Tower and the area under it, a total of 34 acres. They then began an ambitious development which opened as the Tower City complex in March, 1991. It includes a Skylight Office Tower, a Chemical Bank Office Tower, a Ritz Carlton Hotel, almost 100 stores and restaurants and an eleven screen movie theatre complex.

The newly remodeled rapid transit station below Tower City, already a hub of activity, will be even more utilized once a special connection to the Gateway sports center is completed.

A second phase of Tower City hopes to add a department store, shops and restaurants all the way to the banks of the Cuyahoga River. It appears the venerable old landmark is returning to its former glory.

# IV.
# ELIOT NESS

## The famed Untouchable spent the best years of his life right here in Cleveland

Assistant Cuyahoga County prosecutor Charles McNamee stomped his feet to ward off the cold as the sun began to set on a late January afternoon in 1936. McNamee swallowed hard, nodded to his men and began his deliberate march toward the enterance of the Harvard Club, a gambling casino just south of Cleveland's city limits in Newburg Heights.

McNamee, his two assistants and ten private detectives from the McGrath Detective Agency, were going to close down the joint, an unheard of practice at the time since the infamous Cleveland Syndicate controlled not only the city but the police department as well. It was for that reason McNamee bypassed the local law enforcement agencies and deputized the detectives.

"This is a raid," McNamee announced to a burly doorman at the club's entrance. "You better step aside," he added, flashing his search warrant.

"Oh no you don't," the doorman growled, pushing the prosecutor. The doorway was a mass of jostling humanity as an indignant Shimmy Patton, the club's operator, appeared.

"What the hell is going on?" he asked in amazement.

"I've got a search and seizure warrant for this place," McNamee boldly announced.

"The hell you do. Where's that goddam Cullitan (the county prosecutor)?" Patton asked, jabbing a finger into McNamee's chest.

"He's closing down the Thomas Club," McNamee answered, referring to a similar casino raid in another suburb.

Patton was furious. His short, portly frame shook with anger. He demanded to know why he had not been tipped off.

Although the assistant prosecutor did not know it at the time, Shimmy Patton's agitation was not because of the gambling raid, he could always bribe his way out of that trouble. The problem was that hiding out in the club

*Ness' boyish grin earned him the nickname "boy scout."*

that same night was the FBI's public enemy number one, the notorious Alvin Karpis.

"You fellows are prosecutors," Patton shouted. "You just step aside and let those other fellows you've got with you try to get in here, we'll mow 'em down." He gestured to the cold, steel gun barrels his men had already pulled from their coats.

McNamee paused, surveyed the crowd of gamblers inside who were just beginning to understand what was going on, looked up at the ring of gunmen staring down from the balcony above and quickly decided that discretion was the better part of valor.

"I don't want any bloodshed," the prosecutor said. "I'll give you half an hour to get these people out of here. Then we're coming back."

As McNamee withdrew to confer with his men in the parking lot by the club's entrance, inside the Harvard Club all hell broke loose. In the rush to escape tables fell, money scattered and customers helped themselves to the loot on their way out the door.

As the sky darkened County Prosecutor Frank Cullitan, fresh from the Thomas Club raid, arrived with more detectives. There Cullitan had reacted to a similar show of resistance by smashing a park bench through the door, confiscating two truck loads of gambling paraphernalia, $1000 in change and a small weapons cache.

Patton, supervising the mass exit in a dark hat and black overcoat, spotted Cullitan's arrival. He rushed over, his white scarf blowing in the breeze.

"Anyone who goes in there gets his head blown off," he shouted. "You've got your goddam homes to protect, I've got my goddam business to protect."

"I've tried every decent way I could," Cullitan shouted back.

"No you haven't," Patton cut him off.

"It's my job to close this place."

"Why don't you quit your job?"

"I'm going to see this through."

Patton stormed back inside. He turned off the parking lot's lights, leaving the public officials in a cold, eerie darkness. Cullitan crossed Harvard Avenue to use a gas station's telephone.

He called County Sheriff John Sulzmann. His chief jailer, William Murphy, answered the phone. "I'm out at the Harvard Club and I need some help," Cullitan explained. "Send out 10-20 deputies, all you can get."

"The sheriff's sick in bed," Murphy answered. "I'll have to call you back."

A few minutes later the phone rang, Murphy again. "The sheriff says he's sticking to his home-rule policy. He won't send no one out there unless the Mayor of Newburg Heights asks him."

Since the illegal casino operated openly for five years there was little hope of cooperation from the Newburg Heights officials. Cullitan tried calling Cleveland's police chief, George Matowitz, but he wasn't in either.

Out of desperation he decided to place one last call. Cleveland's new Safety Director had a reputation as somewhat of a gangbuster. Cullitan reached him in the middle of a city council meeting. He promised to come right out.

An hour later it was nearing 11 o'clock, six hours since McNamee first tried to go inside. His men were becoming restless. About 300 spectators mulled around the street.

Suddenly they heard a siren in the distance. No, there was more than one. It was a symphony of police sirens speeding down Harvard Avenue. Twenty uniformed patrolmen, four plain clothes detectives and a fireman spilled out of a string of squad cars. Ten motorcycle cops dismounted. They surrounded a tall, slight figure in a camel's hair topcoat with a gold "City of Cleveland — Director of Public Safety" badge on his lapel.

"Let's have a light here," he spoke quickly and quietly. "All right, let's go."

Unarmed, the Safety Director led a small army carrying sawed-off shotguns, tear gas pistols and revolvers up to the Harvard Club's steel door.

"I'm Eliot Ness," he told a pair of eyes staring at him through the peephole. "I'm coming in with some search warrants."

A few anxious moments later the door slowly swung open. "All right," he told Cullitan. "Let your men go in there and serve your warrants. We'll back them up."

Fortunately for Ness the only backing up they had to do was break up a fist fight that developed when one of Patton's men tried to smash a newspaper photographer's camera. Newburg Heights was out of his jurisdiction. After answering Cullitan's call for help he had hurried over to Central Police station to round up a posse, explaining that they'd be acting as private citizens once they crossed the city limits.

Although the county prosecutors accomplished goal of closing down the club without bloodshed, it it was no gambling raid to write home about. Only a huge racetrack blackboard and an U-shaped blackjack table remained in the stripped out hall. All the roulette wheels, slot machines and crap tables were carted away in large furniture vans during the stalemate. Club operators Shimmy Patton and Arthur Hebebrand escaped out the back window to reopen the club in Portage County. Alvin Karpis also escaped.

But for Cleveland's new Safety Director, whose rosy cheeks, boyish grin and deceivingly naive manner already earned him the knickname "boy-scout," it was a tremendous publicity coup. Maybe there was something to those stories about him and Al Capone after all.

Except for occasional displays of raw courage like the Harvard Club raid, Eliot Ness' only similarity to television's Robert Stack, the gun-on-the-hip gang buster of "The Untouchables" series, was a certain facial resemblence. The real Eliot Ness was a charming, soft-spoken, unpretentious college graduate

*The Harvard Club Raid: Ness (second from right) confers with county prosecutors moments before entering the club.*

who enjoyed boating, tennis, cats, women and scotch. A dedicated law enforcement officer, on the job he was a tight-lipped interrogator speaking in authoritative, short, terse phrases. "He could say NO so pleasantly yet mean it so forcefully," James Livingstone, his police secretary, recalled.

Among close friends he liked to kick off his shoes, relax and unleash his bubbling sense of humor. He seldom carried a gun, his philosphy being: "They won't be so quick to shoot at you if they know you can't shoot back." Preferring the more diplomatic approach, he felt he failed if he had to resort to the use of a weapon.

Eliot Ness was born on April 19, 1902. He grew up on Chicago's South Side, the youngest of five children of a Norwegian immigrant couple, Peter and Emma Ness. His parents named him after the author of *Silas Marner*, George Eliot, probably unaware the name was a pseudonym for Mary Ann Evans. More than 10 years younger than his brother and sisters, Eliot was doted upon as a child. He first became interested in detective work as an avid reader of Sherlock Holmes.

In later years Ness boasted that his father was an honest baker of moderate means "who never cheated anyone out of a nickel." He liked to tell a story about a man who once asked his father to bake a cake in the shape of an M. The next day the man came back and said, "No, I meant a *fancy* M." His father threw the cake away and gave it another try. The following day the man returned to discover an ornate M-shaped cake of an unusual script.

"That's more like it," he smiled.

"Should I wrap it up?" the elder Ness asked proudly.

"No thanks, I'll eat it here."

Peter Ness' fortunes flucuated, but they were on the upswing by the time Eliot graduated from high school. He studied political science, commerce and business administration at the University of Chicago and received his degree in 1925. His family could not understand why a young man with his excellent education and optimistic nature would choose a career in law enforcement. "Someone has to do it," he would answer.

After a brief stint checking insurance claims for a retail credit company he joined the U.S. Prohibition Bureau in 1929. Prohibition was a decade-long experiment that did more to foster crime in America than anything before or since. Chicago's police force,

*Eliot Ness, man-about-town.*

as in most of the nation's big cities, was dominated by the man who could provide the thirsty citizens with bootleg beer — scarfaced Al Capone, the underworld's most powerful figure.

On his first assignment Ness discovered that the Prohibition Bureau was not much different from the police force. Ted Kuhn, a retired Chicago Prohibition agent, remembered Ness was excited about a still he'd found; he wanted to raid it.

"Did you tell anyone about it?" Kuhn asked.

"Just a couple guys," the young rookie answered.

"Then we'd better get a warrant right away."

By the time they got to the still it was already abandoned, although they did confiscate a large supply of mash.

Ness was given the opportunity to do something about the situation when his brother-in-law, Alexander Jamie, quit the Justice Department to become chief investigator for "The Secret Six," an organization of Chicago businessmen who were trying to break Capone's grip on the city. They helped Ness assemble within the Prohibition Bureau a hand-picked team of investigators (The Untouchables) who were immune to Capone's hefty payoffs. Ness was put in charge at the tender age of 27 because it had been his idea to create the special unit. Besides, Jamie could trust him with his secret contacts.

Ness received a great deal of publicity when he attached a steel blade to the front of a truck, put on a football helmet and bulldozed into Capone's breweries. After two years of smashing stills and investigating Capone's activities, Ness was finally successful in building a case against the mobster on, of all things, income tax evasion. The once invincible Capone was convicted and sent to prison.

In 1933, the 21st amendment repealed Prohibition but the bootleg industry continued to prosper by circumventing the taxation that came with legalization. Ness, by this time married to Edna Staley, Jamie's secretary, was transferred first to the Treasury Department's Alcohol Tax Unit (ATU) in Cincinnati, and in the fall of 1934, to Cleveland to concentrate on the illegal liquor coming in from Canada.

He was happy to come here, confessing to his third wife, Betty, in later years that the most frightening period of his career had been in Cincinnati going up against Appalachian moonshiners who did not think twice about picking off a "revenooer." (The worldly Chicago gangsters had been a bit more cautious about hurting a federal agent.)

As chief investigator for the Enforcement branch of the ATU, Ness began knocking off Cleveland's stills at a rate of one a day. Within a month he was tipped off that molasses was flowing into the Cuyahoga River from a warehouse beneath the High-Level bridge. He immediately raided the place. Some of his men dropped through the skylight and slipped in by the fire escape while others barged through the front door. To their amazement, they discovered a four-story still, worth $20,000 in parts alone. One of the largest ever raided anywhere, it was manned by a lone fireman tending to the boiler in the basement. Ness decided to try a tactic he had once employed in Chicago to find out who controlled the operation. He closed the door and waited inside until six more workers showed up.

On another occasion his men took over the offices of a bootleg business on the East Side and for the next four hours answered telephone calls complaining about late deliveries. They compiled a list of 300 drinking spots buying the illegal brew. On that list were the names of many prominent Clevelanders.

Ness' success began to show in the rapid rise of legal liquor sales and the higher price of illegal liquor. Yet, excluding the bootleggers, few Clevelanders realized Ness' presence until Republican Harold Burton was elected mayor on a "reform" ticket in 1935.

One of Burton's main campaign issues was the widespread corruption that had crept into city hall during Prohibition. He had pledged to clean it up and was looking around for a safety director who could do the job.

About this time *Plain Dealer* reporter Wes Lawrence was transferred from the federal beat, where he had been covering Ness, to city hall. One of *The Plain Dealer*'s editors suggested to Lawrence that the mayor should consider Ness for a job. Lawrence in turn suggested to Burton that Ness might be a candidate for safety director, but did not expect anything to come of it because of Eliot's lack of local political connections. Actually, his out-of-town background made him all the more appealing to Burton. Learning that Ness had become known as an "Untouchable" in Chicago after turning down a $2,000-a-week bribe while earning only $2,800 a year, Burton was convinced he had found his man. Ness, eager for a new challenge after six years of chasing bootleggers, accepted the position on the condition that he be given complete freedom to pursue his own investigations. On December 11, 1935, the city's newspapers bannered a new chapter in Cleveland's history.

I'LL ACT FIRST THEN TALK — NESS.

"I hope to take necessary action first and talk about it later," he told newsmen.

### CLEVELAND: MEET THE MAN WHO BROKE CAPONE

"Six feet and 172 pounds of fight and vigor, an expert criminologist who looks like a collegian but can battle crime with the best of them, today accepted the job of upholding law and order in Cleveland."

At 33 he was the youngest safety director in the city's history. With his Scandinavian good looks, grey-blue eyes and brown hair parted in the middle, Ness captured the public's imagination. Wearing the latest double-breasted suits and living with his attractive wife in Bay Village, Ness was the dynamic symbol that Depression-weary Cleveland newspaper readers needed.

Two days after his appointment the new safety director was already changing policy. He joined Traffic Commissioner Edward Donahue in urging the traffic police to practice salesmanship and courtesy instead of "the big stick," expecially in a convention city like Cleveland. In 1936 Cleveland would host some 200 conventions, including those of the Republican National Party and the American Legion. The Great Lakes Exposition would draw over seven million visitors in 1936-37.

The newspapers covered him touring the police precincts, dropping in on the "Roaring Third" (East 33rd at Longwood) at 3 a.m., watching his men track down a burglar in the Williamson Building or his firemen battle a warehouse blaze. Yet, more important things were happening behind the scenes.

Ness quickly learned the deplorable condition of the city's safety department equipment: police revolvers with tobacco stuck in the firing chambers from too much time spent in the officers' pockets; fire hoses that did not fit the hydrants; one hook-and-ladder so old it could only climb a hill in reverse gear.

Ness realized, however, that the greatest obstacle to his effectiveness was the quality of the local police force. Therefore, he sat down with Prosecutor Cullitan to plan his strategy.

"We start with the police force," Ness said.

"It's going to be hard getting evidence against the police," Cullitan warned. "Most gangsters are loathe to put the finger on a cop. They're afraid of retaliation."

"Any offender coming forth to testify against the police will be granted immunity from prosecution as well as protection against retaliation," Ness stated as he paced the floor of Cullitan's office. "We're going to promise them both. We're going to contact every known offender in this city if we have to go back to 1920. Any offender who will come forth will get both immunity and protection. In fact, my people are already at work."

Cleveland's police department was in such bad shape some policemen actually doubled as enforcers for the very gangsters they were supposed to be investigating. Such payoffs were the reason for Ness' crackdown on the professional gamblers. He was actually quite liberal in his gambling views, but it was the $200,000 illegal weekly take put in the hands of criminals that concerned him.

Ness needed a Cleveland group of Untouchables. He recruited Keith Wilson, a fellow ATU investigator who would later become a judge in Chicago. Next came Tom Clothey, who had worked with Ness' nephew, Wallace Jamie, on probing a corrupt police department in St. Paul, Minnesota. Dick Jones, a federal agent, was brought in from Chicago. Ness appointed attorney Robert Chamberlin, a Bay Village neighbor whom he had taken along on a few raids, as his administrative assistant.

A coalition of Cleveland merchants similar to Chicago's Secret Six raised money to supplement the salaries of Ness' undercover men, who were on the city's payroll as laborers. The fund was also used

*Above: Mayor Harold Burton (left) shows Ness his new red, white and blue police cars. Below: Ness inspects the new motorcycles for his traffic unit.*

for other activities, including payments for informers and travel expenses.

Ness' program was not calculated to ingratiate him with the police department. In his first month he broke up many cozy arrangements by transferring 28 lieutenants, half the force's 126 sergeants and 400 of the 1,151 patrolmen. He then fired two veteran officers for drunkenness on duty.

His private investigators were also turning up evidence of police corruption. William Burton, the mayor's son, who worked for Ness during his 1936 summer vacation, recalled staking out a bookie joint on Woodland Avenue. "Three minutes after we called the precinct station for a raid, people began jumping out the windows," said Burton, today a Cleveland lawyer. "Everyone was gone by the time the cops arrived." In the future, Ness used officers from outside precincts for his raids.

Clayton Fritchey, a nationally syndicated columnist who was a *Press* reporter at the time, provided Ness with a needed break. A reader had tipped off Fritchey to a cemetery lot investment racket that was bilking many of Cleveland's foreign-born residents through the sale of phony grave certificates. Fritchey ran across the name of a mysterious John L. Dacek, who owned $80,000 in cemetery lot "investments." Given to comtemplating anagrams, Fritchey awoke in the middle of the night, struck by the similarity of the name to that of Captain Louis J. Cadek, whom he had seen that day at City Hall. He consulted Ness, whose colorful exploits were already earning him trusting friendships with newsmen, and the safety director immediately turned his barrage of wiretaps, informants and bank account investigations in Cadek's direction.

Cadek was one of the most notorious police officials in town. He once threw a party for some local bootleggers. In the middle of the room he placed an empty barrel; by the end of the evening it was filled with cash. He had deposited over $100,000 in the bank in three years on a policeman's salary of $3,500!

The key witness in this case was the brother of a petty bootlegger whom Cadek had turned over to federal agents after he missed a couple of payoffs. After his arrest Cadek began "to sing" about others on the force.

The Cadek case was the beginning of an amalgamation of Fritchey's connections and Ness' investigative forces. *Press* editor Louis B. Seltzer let Fritchey work with him full time, thereby giving his paper the edge in scoops while at the same time providing Ness with an extra investigator.

In June 1936, Ness led a raid on a bookie joint at the Black Hawk Night Club on Ivanhoe Road. As police were gathering evidence, Edward Harwood walked in to collect the rent for his father, Michael.

"You can't raid this place," he told Ness not realizing who he was. "My old man's the police captain in this district."

A three-month investigation revealed that Harwood owned a string of restaurants, night clubs and taverns. Ness' men obtained a staggering array of testimony from bootleggers, speakeasy operators, gamblers and madams who paid Harwood's men for protection. Harwood was like Cadek in one respect: If the payments stopped, the protection stopped. Ness transferred all the police assigned to the East 185th and Nottingham station and was able to obtain indictments against Harwood, a deputy inspector, two lieutenants, a sergeant and three officers. They were all eventually tried and convicted.

In other instances, to avoid a cumbersome court case, Ness merely confronted the individual corrupt cop with evidence and demanded his resignation.

Ness did not believe that quantity could substitute for quality in police work. He once explained to his friend Dan Moore, now the director of a public speaker service here, that if the number of police went below a certain percentage of the population you had a crime wave and if the number went above it you had a police state. What Ness hoped to do was replace the old guard with a new breed of law enforcement officer.

He swore in 10 rookies with this advice: "If people have been accustomed to giving you things for nothing prior to your becoming a policeman, I suppose it's all right for you to continue to accept those things. However, if people who never gave you anything for free before now want to give you something without charge, you can conclude they are buying your badge and uniform."

Insulted by the public's image of a policeman as a "Flatfoot dimwit," Ness once told the League of Women Voters that a good officer should be a marksman, a boxer, a wrestler, a sprinter, a diplomat, a memory expert and an authority on various subjects.

Since his own career had begun with a few postgraduate criminolgy courses at the University of Chicago, Ness sent Lieutenant Patrick Lenahan to the FBI training school. He returned to set up Cleveland's first police academy. A rookie previously had been given a week's instruction, then put on a beat with a veteran. Lenahan inaugurated a three month training program which included such subjects as approach psychology, arrest procedure, criminal law and first aid. He also required at least a high school diploma for candidates. The Civil Service qualifying exam was made harder. Only 100 out of the thousand or more who took it passed.

Ness used the test result list in making his appointments. He passed up candidates *only* if something untoward showed up in their background. Richard Wagner, a member of that orignal training class, later became police chief. He remembers Ness' personal instructions: "Here's my private phone number. If anyone asks you for any money at any time, call me immediately. If you do get asked and don't call me, don't plan on being a police officer for very long."

Prior to Ness' taking office, police department appointments and promotions had been bought at escalating prices. The new Eliot Ness "book policemen" were ribbed by veterans, especially after the safety director added extra points to the promotional exam for marksmanship to compensate for the extra points given for seniority. He was nudging his younger appointees up through the ranks.

Corrupt cops were just one of Ness' concerns. Labor racketeers were another. They were scaring away out-of-town developers at a time when Cleveland could least afford it. Harry Barrington, a business agent for the Carpenters Union, made the mistake of punching Hubert Cornwell, a home builder he was blackmailing. Cornwell went to Ness, who found 39 other contractors ready to testify against Barrington.

Barrington's modus operandi was crude but lucrative. He and Al Ruddy, president of the Carpenters District Council, would approach a builder, claim a "technical violation" and demand money by threatening to pull the union help off the job. If that didn't work, they resorted to vandalism.

Barrington was indicted, but out on bond fled to Los Angeles, where Ness' men tracked him down. Ruddy then promised Barrington that if he pleaded guilty to avoid a trial Ruddy would have him out in six months. Barrington agreed. But finding himself in jail three years later, he made a deal with Ness to

turn state's evidence against Ruddy, who was convicted of extortion and sent to prison in 1940.

Ness used the Barrington plea to ask the public to report to him any evidence of blackmail or extortion. He really wanted Don Campbell, president of Painters District Council, and John McGee, business agent for the Glaziers Union. They had risen to power on a wave of window-smashing terrorism. In 1934 a permanent police tail was placed on the duo, who delighted in taunting their followers with long rides in the country and wild chases through the city's back alleys.

The ultimate caper, however, took place on a sunny spring day when they rented a pair of Packard convertibles, placed an accordian player and a saxophone player in the first one, then sat on the back seat of the second one dressed in top hats, striped trousers and cutaway coats. They led a dilapidated police cruiser down Euclid Avenue during the height of the noonday rush. The band played "Me and My Shadow" as side placards announced McGEE AND CAMPBELL COMEDY CIRCUS — ANIMATED BY THE CLEVELAND NEWSPAPERS AND POLICE DEPARTMENT.

The cops retaliated by throwing the pair in jail on a Friday night so they would have to wait until Monday for the courts to open and packed their cell

*Ness at his desk.*

with a smelly collection of tramps.

Three years after Campbell and McGee's weekend visit Ness was still trying to arrange a more permanent stay in jail for the pair. Like Barrington, they used the threat of a "jurisdictional dispute" to stall a project. Since glass installation was the final stage in constructing a building, anxious contractors usually acquiesced to their demands. Uncooperative businesses found their windows smashed.

On March 8, 1938, a year after the investigation began, Campbell and McGee were found guilty of extorting $1,200 from restauranteur Vernon Stouffer after threatening to block renovation of his Playhouse Square restaurant. Ness' reputation was so imtimidating that the defense lawyers protested against his sitting in the courtroom with the prosecutors.

The convictions of the union officials were reported in newspapers across the country.

The labor racketeering investigations were a great boost for Ness' career, but they had exacted a toll. His life had been repeatedly threatened, and a bodyguard had to be assigned to him around the clock. William F. McCarthy, the former chief of the liquidation division of the Small Business Administration, who was a police prosecutor at the time, remembered Ness being shot at as he drove along the Shoreway.

*Ness' second wife, Evaline.*

Although the threats had little personal effect on Ness — he was as relaxed and jovial as ever among close friends — they caused his wife to live in almost constant fear. Though she hid her misgivings about his career from Eliot, she once confessed to a friend that if she ever thought her fears were holding him back she would leave him. Early the following year she asked him for a divorce, which he readily granted. The divorce added grist to the chatter about Ness' swinging social life.

Friends recall that Ness was concerned that the divorce might affect his reputation in Cleveland and at one time even considered resigning as safety director. He was very particular about his reputation and tried to maintain an image of probity. This attitude would later get him into some trouble.

Ness did not remain single long, however, and in 1938 married Evaline McAndrews, an artist and model, whom he had met casually on a train to Minneapolis a few years before. She had moved to Cleveland prior to the marriage and worked at Higbee's as a fashion illustrator.

Now a resident of Palm Beach, Florida, Evaline Ness, who retains her name for professional purposes, is remarried and enjoys her work as an illustrator of children's books. She and Eliot were divorced in 1946.

Evaline Ness recalled those days in Cleveland, noting that Eliot enjoyed the limelight. "That may have been the best part of his life," she said. "He never really talked much about what he was doing. We'd go out at night and have a good time, but there would never be any talk about his work."

It was a halcyon time for lawmen, who suddenly found themselves glorified as never before. Movies like *G-Men*, starring James Cagney, made legends of law enforcement officials.

The newspapers, of course, were filled with tales of public enemies like John Dillinger and FBI agents like Melvin Purvis. Because of his exploits in Chicago, Ness ranked high with newspapermen here as a source of good copy. And women were attracted by his good looks and considerate manner; at a time when a mere wink in public was enough to raise eyebrows among Cleveland's conservative populous, Ness openly enjoyed their company.

Prior to his second marriage, his midnight swims and dawn motorboat rides at the Clifton Lagoon boathouse, once owned by automobile manufacturer Alexander Winton, caused tongues to wag.

Evaline Ness recalled that Monday nights, after city council meetings, were particularly festive times at the Lakewood boathouse, to which Ness had moved from Bay Village. Eliot was good company in a group of newspapermen and politicians and could drink all night with his friends and arrive fresh at the office the next day.

Ness was not a loud man, even after considerable drink, and spoke softly; he had a quiet laugh that was almost inaudible. He liked sports, particularly tennis, and worked at keeping trim.

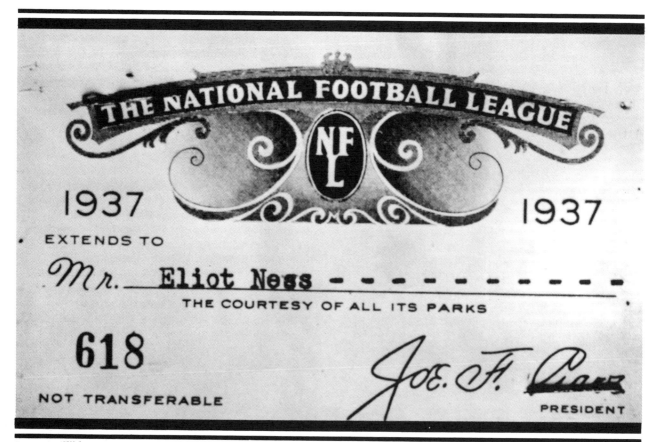

*Every football fan's dream come true, a pass to every park in the NFL.*

While Ness enjoyed money, he spent it freely on good times and automobiles. He liked to surprise Evaline by driving up to the boathouse with a new car for her.

Ironically, he liked the company of wealthy persons, and in fact was somewhat awed by them during his Cleveland days. He had an antenna for phonies, though, and avoided them, rich or poor. As a businessman, he was naive and later in life he would suffer from this lack of sophistication.

When he was first approached for the safety director's job he speculated that it would probably be "lots of fun." He managed to mix business and pleasure while tracking down leads across the city's landscape. One night he stopped at an east side bar with Ted Kuhn, the Chicago Prohibition agent who had come to Cleveland. Ness tried to question the bartender but kept getting "I don't know anything." Suddenly a customer ran up excitedly and told the bartender he had hit the jackpot on the Paces Races pinball machine. He wanted to trade the slugs in for money. Ness told his driver to call the station and have his men come take out the Paces Races machine, which was illegal.

"Who are you?" the bartender asked.

"I'm Eliot Ness, the safety director."

"No you're not," a drunken customer butted in. "I know him personally and you're not him."

"If you don't believe me," Ness told the bartender as he was leaving, "ask the cop who's been hiding in the corner since we came in. His drink is still at the bar."

Ness' youthful appearance produced a somewhat similar reaction on another occasion. Stepping into a rollicking bar on Fleet Avenue with young Bud Burton, a *News* reporter, Ness in his usual reserved manner told the bartender he would like to ask him some questions.

"And who the hell are you?" demanded the bartender.

"I'm Eliot Ness and this is Mr. Burton."

"Hey," the bartender bellowed, interrupting the festivities, "get a load of these two. They're so drunk they think they're the safety director and mayor!"

On another occasion Ness asked Ohio Governor Martin L. Davey and Dan Moore, then head of the state's securities office, to meet him for a drink. As a joke, Ness had arranged for an actor to come into the bar and pass himself off as a drug pusher.

In the course of the evening the actor began to get more involved in his role, even starting a fight with a bystander. The unsuspecting governor became more and more nervous and finally bolted in fear that the place would be raided, making his exit down a fire escape.

Ness also prided himself on his physical condition. His slight build belied a powerful set of arm and chest muscles developed during one youthful summer he had spent working in an auto plant dipping auto radiators. He constantly did pushups, occasionally smoked cigars but disdained cigarettes altogether. Before lunch he often would visit Dewey Mitchell's Health Club in the Standard Building for session of jujitsu or handball.

*Ness playing badminton at Dewey Mitchell's Health Club in the Standard Building.*

Despite his outward composure, Ness was a shy, nervous man. He bit his fingernails to the quick and constantly picked at his thumb with an index finger until the skin was shaved away.

Ness kept his emotions contained. "He was the most controlled man I ever met," recalled Evaline Ness.

Mentally, he enjoyed psychological thrusts and parries and considered it of prime importance that he carry himself in such a way that he be underestimated. He felt that in this way he could keep people off balance. Thus, he rarely carried a weapon. His tastes were simple. He never ate salads, vegetables or spiced foods. His diet consisted almost exclusively of meat and potatoes. His stomach was so sensitive that once when he opened a kitchen drawer in which a spice jar had broken open, the smell made him ill.

He had been brought up in a Christian Scientist family, but did not practice the religion. Yet he had a tendency to shrug off injury and illness and was not overly sympathetic with those who complained of ailing.

During the 1930s, dining and dancing at lunch was in vogue for those who could afford it. Downtown Cleveland thrived with places like the Lotus Gardens and the Golden Pheasant which featured big-name bands. Despite his image as a police officer, Ness was not above participating in the noontime gaiety.

Since he had no children at the time, Ness' home life was minimal. He did not particularly care for movies, so in the evening he might close up the Bronze Room at the Cleveland Hotel or the Vogue Room of the old Hollenden. His touring of the city 16 hours a day made him a popular figure and frankly, was a factor in Mayor Burton's reelection.

Yet, it did have its disadvantages. He once confided to his lawyer friend, John Butler, that he had to be careful of what he said. "Anything I whisper to a friend comes out in the papers the next day as if I'd shouted it from a megaphone on Public Square." One of his diversions in the Thirties was touring the banquet circuit to explain his activities. He would ask someone in the audience to call a policeman and then time how fast the officer got there. Ness could expect a speedy response because by 1938 he had modernized Cleveland's police department, replacing the old foot-beat, call-box, jump-on-a-streetcar system with a motorized fleet dispatched by two-way radios.

Ness reformed the police department in many

*Mayor Burton (center left), flanked by Ness and Police chief George Matowitz, host the Illinois police in Ness' office during the Great Lakes Exposition, 1936.*

ways. He cleaned up much of the corruption, certainly. But he also instituted new squads, such as a juvenile unit, to nip crime where he believed it all began — in the youthful bud. He also devoted much time to streamlining the traffic division, cutting down on accidents. One year Cleveland highways were called the safest in the nation by the National Safety Council.

In later years Ness was successful, too, at an equally difficult undertaking, one that involved organized crime. After the repeal of Prohibition, the Mayfield Road Gang, the strong-arm branch of the Cleveland Syndicate, had turned its attention toward extortion and was once again making its weight felt in town. According to Hank Messick's book, *The Silent Syndicate*, organized crime in Cleveland was controlled by four of the founding fathers of the national crime syndicate: Moe Dalitz, Sam Tucker, Louis Rothkopf and Morris Kleinman. While the Mayfield Road Gang gained all the publicity with their bloody tactics, the Big Four amassed a huge fortune in bootleg money behind the scenes in a more sophisticated manner.

When Ness and Cullitan closed down the syndicate's lucrative post-Prohibition casino interests in Cuyahoga County, they were forced to move first to the outlying counties, then down to Kentucky, and finally to Miami Beach, Las Vegas and Havana, Cuba.

The Mayfield Road Gang, meanwhile, was moving into the local numbers racket through a

calculated campaign of murders and threats. In the 1920s the numbers game had been a small if quite profitable operation confined to the city's black community. But by the time Ness arrived on the scene, the Mayfield Road Gang had already taken control of the racket, forcing the many independent operators to fork over to Big Angelo Lonardo a sizeable amount of their take. Big Angelo had inherited control of the mob from his father, who had been assassinated during the internecine gang wars of the Twenties.

Ness hardly expected to wipe out numbers betting in Cleveland. He simply wanted to limit it, fearing the Mayfield Road Gang would only muscle into other areas of the community if the law got a stranglehold on numbers. The independent number operators, however, were reticent about asking for police protection, since they were pushing an illegal game in the first place.

As usual, Ness pursued the greater of the two evils. In this case it was the leaders of the Mayfield Road Gang, the operatives of organized crime.

He went after lesser law violators in stranger ways. Once a young man whose father operated a still was told to report to the safety director's office. Visibly shaking, he stepped inside. After a few seconds Ness looked up from his desk and said, "Your father is using too much sugar." The young man returned home to close down his father's still. It was part of Ness' style.

On April 1, 1939, after more than three years of

work by a small core of black policemen and police-women, 23 indictments for blackmail and running policy houses were brought against the gang's leaders, including Big Angelo Lonardo and Alex (Shondor) Birns. Tipped off to the secret indictments, the gang scattered across the country. It would take Detective Martin Cooney some two years to bring them back from as far away as Mexico for trial.

Ness would not take a case to court unless he was confident of a conviction. Since he could also count on editorial support from the local news media, few indictments brought in by his men ever failed. The most notable exception was the late Shondor Birns.

Birns, who was blown up in his car in 1975, escaped standing trial with the rest of the Mayfield Road Gang by perfectly timing a hernia operation. At his own trial Birns tricked the prosection's star witness, who had been kept in hiding for three years in Philadelphia, into identifying his lawyer by mistake. Birns' lawyer, who looked and dressed like him, had switched seats with Birns during the court's lunch recess. Shondor Birns went on to plague the city's police department for many years.

The Mayfield Road Gang indictments marked the end of Ness' major investigations. In a little over four years he had completely revamped the city's safety forces, intimidated the major labor racketeers, started a police academy, cut juvenile delinquency by 80 percent and won the National Safety Award for the city's traffic record.

In 1940, Mayor Burton, who owed much of his success to Ness and vice versa, won a seat in the U.S. Senate and appointed Edward Blythin, an assistant law director, to replace him as a ten-month interim mayor. There was much speculation that Blythin would agree to step down in 1941 and pave the way for Ness' candidacy. That fall two of Ness' Democratic friends, Judge Frank Lausche and *Plain Dealer* political writer Ralph Kelly, met at the safety director's apartment to discuss the upcoming mayoral campaign. "I suggested that Eliot run," Lausche recalled. "But he didn't want to. He insisted I run."

Evaline Ness recalled that when they would get together with Lausche and his wife, Jan, the two men would play a game of mayor. "Eliot would tell Frank that he ought to run for mayor and Frank would insist that Eliot run. I never thought that Eliot was seriously interested in politics. He was not a political person."

Lausche ran and won the election by an even greater majority than Burton's record landslide. However, his decision to keep Ness, a holdover from a Republican administration, sparked a feud with local Democratic party chief Ray T. Miller.

Miller, representing Cleveland's large labor union faction, had made a campaign issue out of bringing in "a real G-man" as safety director. He was referring to the fact that Ness, an ex-Treasury and Prohibition agent, was often mistakenly identified as a former

FBI agent. His labor rackets investigations, his publicizing of a Teamster's extortion racket at the Northern Ohio Food Terminal, and the impossible task of trying to keep order during two of the bloodiest strikes of the Thirties — Fisher Body and Republic Steel — all combined to make Ness unpopular among the city's labor leaders.

It was also claimed his labor bureau was being used to spy on the unions, a charge which arose from his obeying J. Edgar Hoover's directive to protect Cleveland's many defense plants from possible sabotage in the event of war.

Although the police department had a reputation for protecting management and not labor, Ness tried to be fair in his dealings with the developing union movement. Ness, in fact, once told management at the Fisher Body strike to disarm the plant police or he would pull his own men out.

Lausche's refusal to remove Ness, in a show of independence that would come to characterize his later career as Ohio governor and U.S. Senator, caused enough turmoil within his young Democratic administration to make Ness uncomfortable. The safety director also came under attack for spending too much time away from the city, battling venereal disease on the nation's army's bases for the Federal Security Agency, a job he first took as a volunteer when the World War II troop build-up began. He defended his federal job by citing New York Mayor Fiorello LaGuardia's dual role as the nation's civil defense chief.

Other factors began adding to a growing un-pleasantness within the safety director's office. For one thing he was bored. In six years he had done about everything there was to do. A new plan giving the police and fire chiefs greater leeway in granting civil service promotions was met with stiff opposition within the ranks. The Civil Service Commission was pressuring Ness to remove the undercover men that were hidden on the city's payroll as laborers. His private fund dried up once he began investigating ambulance-chasing lawyers instead of labor rack-eteers. He complained that his squad cars were in as terrible shape as his men from being driven around all day.

Meanwhile, his traffic safety record was being threatened by Natural Death Incorporated, an insurance racket whereby investors took out up to 100 policies on a chronic alcoholic. Investors kept them supplied with "canned heat" (cheap liquor) until they either burned out or were hit by a car, sometimes intentionally.

Ness helped *Press* reporter Clayton Fritchey and state insurance investigator Gaspar Corso obtain the necessary records from publicity-shy companies to convict a woman speculator who had inherited the business from her mother. Once Ness had shown that the business involved risk of felony, the speculators dried up.

One source of enjoyment for Ness during this period was his interest in radio. Wayne Mack, local

*Ness (on right) doing a radio stint on WGAR.*

radio performer, started a crime quiz program on WGAR called *Masterminds, Attention!* A group of experts asked questions of witnesses who could only answer "yes" or "no" until the mystery was solved. Ness' keen mind and soft, husky voice disarmed the witnesses so fast, the problems were solved too quickly. Designed to last a half hour each, additional problems were often needed, drying up the suggestions submitted by the listening audience after only 26 weeks. Then one Sunday afternoon the New York Philharmonic concert, which followed Ness' show, was interrupted by news of the Japanese attack on Pearl Harbor.

The war wreaked the same havoc on Ness' life as it did on the rest of the country. It took away his friends. Bob Chamberlin joined the Army, where he rose to the rank of brigadier general. Tom Clothey and Dick Jones joined U.S. Naval Intelligence. Ness' professional life was uncertain and uprooted. But the fatal blow to his Cleveland career was a traffic accident that blemished the image he had always protected so zealously. At 5 a.m. on a cold and snowy March morning in 1942, Ness' car skidded into an oncoming auto on Buckley Avenue. The driver of the other car, Robert Sims, 21, injured his kneecap in the accident.

"I remember the accident," recalled Evaline Ness. "We were coming home from a party and it was icy. I think I was telling Eliot something about a reporter I had told off and we were laughing. It was an ordinary thing. We just slid into the car and the force knocked the breath out of me. Eliot broke his upper plate."

Ness assured Sims he would take care of his hospital expenses, telling the patrolmen who arrived at the scene to keep it under their hats.

The policemen, seeking to cover thenselves, told their captain, who happened to be under investigation by Ness. The accident report was sent downtown and the newspapers were quietly tipped off to the incident. When reporters found the report, two days late and incomplete, the story was big enough to crowd some of the day's war news from page one. Ness, embarrassed by the incident, admitted to having had a few drinks a few hours before the accident, but insisted that it was the icy road conditions that had caused the crash.

"I have never regretted anything more in my life," he told reporters in referring to the cover-up. "I felt I was discharging my duties to the others involved. Obviously, I was trying to avoid publicity."

"I don't think he could stand criticism that well,

*Ness (by window) rented a plane to spot violations of the city's anti-smoke code.*

especially when it came to his job," said Evaline Ness. "That's why he tried to avoid publicity with the accident. It was just one of those things."

The cover-up put an end to his career, many of his friends agreed. Although he had been thinking of resigning, the publicity and the subsequent loss of face hastened his exit.

One month later Ness resigned his position as Cleveland's safety director to devote full time to the Federal Security Agency in Washington. For the next two and a half years he traveled to military bases across the country, combating venereal disease by discouraging prostitution. Labeling VD "Military Saboteur Number One" because of the time and money wasted in treating the disease, Ness used the May Act, a federal law prohibiting prostitution near military bases or recruiting stations, to reduce hookers' business opportunities.

He threatened the industries that thrived on soldiers' paychecks — bars, hotels and cab drivers — with loss of license if found cooperating with the ladies of the evening. If a hooker was arrested, instead of being jailed she was sent to a Civilian Conservation Corps camp for alternative vocational training. At the

same time Ness distributed pamphlets for both men and women on the previously taboo subject. His systematic approach effectively lowered the Army's VD rate.

"Eliot liked that job," Evaline Ness said. "We'd go to all of those small towns and he'd advise them on how to get rid of their red-light districts. We met a lot of funny people in those towns, believe me."

In September of 1944 Ness returned to Cleveland to become chairman of the board of the Diebold Corporation, a company which manufactures safes. The Ralph Rex family, which had substantial holdings in the company, asked Ness to step in and reorganize it. He also became vice president of the Middle East Import-Export Company with his friend Dan Moore. They planned to take advantage of the large amounts of money spent in the area by American soldiers.

As the war drew to a conclusion, so did his second marriage. Eliot and Evaline were divorced, she settling in New York to continue with her art work and he remaining in Cleveland and taking a third wife, Elizabeth Anderson, a sculptress who won many May Show prizes here. Today Betty Ness

*Ness speaking to a neighborhood gathering in 1940.*

*Ness' third wife Betty.*

lives in California.

Settling into the humdrum corporate life of business must have been dificult for Ness to accept after an adult lifetime of headlines. Maybe it was the increasing boredom or maybe the growing insistence of his friend Ralph Kelly, then *The Plain Dealer's* political writer, that made him make a foolish decision — to run for mayor as the Republican candidate in 1947. Looking back, many who knew Ness say that he was forced into the race by his friends, who had overestimated his popularity at this time. Those close to Ness say he was never a very serious political figure and, in the end, the race did nothing but hurt him.

Most of the local Republican party's prominent politicians, the few that there were, had already steered clear of any intention to go up against Mayor Thomas Burke, the popular Democratic incumbent.

The political realities of a Ness race were absurd. Most of the city's Republicans had already fled to the suburbs, leaving a heavily Democratic city behind which still remembered Ness' confrontations with the labor unions.

Buoyed by his friends, and always one for a challenge, especially a challenge that promised a means to regain former glories, an older, heavier Eliot Ness tried to make the transistion from police officer to politico.

But his campaign was doomed from the beginning. The day he announced his candidacy the political analysts in the press wished him the best of luck while at the same time predicting a disaster. The same fickle papers that had supported him so strongly as safety director would not offer the same support to Ness the political candidate. They were already committed to Burke, who, ironically, had been an obscure assistant prosecutor on the night of the Harvard Club raid.

Ness did not expect much at first, telling his wife not to worry, he was not going to win. "He never planned ahead," Betty recalled. "Which suited me just fine. Whatever he did he was doing completely at the time he was doing it. Living with him for 11 years was the most fun I ever had in my life."

As he became more involved in the campaign, Ness somehow began to believe he had a chance. A political novice, he was not a fiery public speaker and never really liked to speak, so he shook hands on Public Square, reminding Clevelanders of what he had accomplished as safety director. He did not grasp the public's short memory. Like a famous ex-athlete, he was barely remembered in his declining years.

In post-World War II America, the GI had replaced the G-man as the country's hero. During an era of economic prosperity people were not interested in a law-and-order candidate. To top it off, Ness had moved from Bratenahl to Wade Park Manor, opening himself to charges of carpetbagging, had been thrice married in a heavily Catholic city and still carried the anti-labor stigma. He tried to campaign as an independent like Burton, by this time a U.S. Supreme Court justice, but it did not work. He was too strongly identified with the monied Republicans. Despite a huge campaign fund, he lost the election by an almost two-to-one ratio, one of the worst defeats in the city's history.

On election night Ness tried to telephone Burke his congratulations in the middle of the victory celebration at the mayor's home. Since Burke and his campaign aides were Ness' friends, they invited him to the party. He accepted, congratulating Burke in person and joining in the festivities. Ness shrugged off the crushing blow by laughing, "Who'd want an honest politician anyway?" It was a sad moment to see Ness, once the toast of the city, a humbled also-ran.

Although he was still interested enough in law enforcement to stop by and visit Al Sutton, Burke's safety director, just to see how things were going, it was difficult for him to get back into his chosen profession. Dan Moore recalls that a Detroit city official once mentioned to him in a telephone conversation that his city was looking for a new police chief. At first the official was delighted at Moore's suggestion that Ness might be the man. A few days later the Detroit official called back to tell Moore he had changed his mind, commenting, "Isn't he the one who, once he gets his name in the papers, runs for mayor?" Positions at the top in law enforcement are rare enough, especially for outsiders, but a

*The last remnant of Ness' glory days was this fading ELIOT NESS FOR MAYOR sign on the side of a deli on East 36th and Cedar Avenue. The building has since been torn down. There is a new effort to name the downtown justice center in his honor.*

reputation for political ambition makes one virtually *persona non grata* in the field.

In many ways the political campaign of 1947 was the last hurrah for Ness, at least during his lifetime. He faded from the public eye and his thoughts turned to business and the propects of a family. In 1949, the couple adopted a three-year-old son, Robert. Parenthood was a new experience for Eliot and he enjoyed it immensely.

But things were not going well in Ness' new-found profession. The ability to recognize a man in the dark by the sound of his footsteps was not a particularly marketable trait in the business world. His new employers tended to use him as a contact man rather than to take advantage of his administrative talents.

Although a great salesman if he believed in something, he did not adjust to the machinations of business or enjoy the rules by which one was forced to conform. Management changes at the Diebold Corporation forced him out and at the same time the Middle East Company that he and Dan Moore had set up began to come apart.

For a time, Eliot took a position with a company that sold frozen hamburger patties, but it was an idea whose time had not yet come and that job petered out, too.

Despite adversity, Eliot and Betty kept their spirits up and remained "partying people," according to their former housekeeper, Corrine Lawson. Entertaining as often as ever, they kept the housekeeper on at almost double the going rate. Sometimes she would catch Eliot ("a meat, potatoes and gravy man") biting his fingernails in concerned solitude. As soon as he was surprised, however, he'd "turn on the sunshine," not wanting to burden others with his troubles.

It was that attitude which caused him problems as president of the Guaranty Paper and Fidelity Check Corporations, the final job that he was destined to hold. "They'd brought him aboard expecting he'd do anything they'd ask," recalled Bill Ayers, who made the move from Cleveland to Coudersport, Pennsylvania with Ness' company in 1956. "But he had the highest principles of anyone I've ever known."

Eliot enjoyed the smalltown life, and enjoyed doting on his son. He became a popular member of the community even though he did not like to hunt or fish like most of his neighbors. "I've seen enough killing in my life," he would tell Betty. He forced her to get rid of her target pistol and shotgun as soon as they were married.

But his financial situation continued to deteriorate. His refusal to use his old connections caused a great deal of strife within the company. As proxy battles threatened to close it down, Ness was forced to borrow money to live on. Feeling that he was failing his family, he became despondent.

While on a trip to New York with Joe Phelps, a friend and bussiness associate, Ness ran into Oscar Fraley, a United Press International reporter. Since Fraley was a former classmate of Phelps, they invited him up to their hotel room for a few drinks.

"You'll have to get Eliot to tell you about his experience as a Prohibition agent in Chicago," Phelps suggested. "He's the guy who dried up Capone. Maybe you've heard of him."

Ness did not ordinarily grab a stranger by the lapels and bore him with stories of his career. But if the occasion arose, he would recall a few memories. Before the two men broke his spell that night the sun was rising. As he left, Fraley suggested that Ness write a book. "You might make some money with it."

"I could use it," Ness remarked.

The next time he was in New York, Fraley, remembering Ness' comment, reminded him of the book idea. "Well, why don't *you* write it?" Ness suggested. The idea fired Fraley to action.

Fraley visited the Ness home in Coudersport. He remembered Ness taking off his shoes, sprawling out on the floor and embroidering newspaper clippings from his scrapbooks with a flowing commentary that mixed wit, perception and warmth. As their work progressed, Ness began to see a light at the end of the tunnel. His spirits lifted.

According to Betty Ness, she and Eliot wrote a rough draft of the book, which would ultimately be titled *The Untouchables*, and Fraley produced the final manuscript. While Ness' exploits against Al Capone and his mob were true accounts, a fictional love story involving Betty and Eliot was intertwined throughout the book.

On a business trip to Cleveland in the spring of 1957, Ness invited his old friend Milton Bowman up to his room at the Pick-Carter Hotel. As he was telling Bowman about his book, which was in the final stages of completion, they were interrupted by a phone call.

"No kidding," Ness remarked just before he hung up.

"What was it?"

"They just told me Hollywood is nibbling on the book idea." Finally, it looked as if good news was on the horizon.

Three weeks later on May 16, 1957, Eliot Ness came home from another difficult day at the financially troubled check company. He stepped into the kitchen and began mixing his customary scotch and soda.

Hearing him come in, his wife called from the garden. When she did not receive an immediate reply, Betty, puzzled, went into the house.

There, sprawled on the kitchen floor, surrounded by melting ice cubes and a puddle of Scotch, lay Eliot Ness, dead from a heart attack. It was 5:15 in the afternoon.

Some time later, his will was read. Ness, the former toast of Cleveland, the swashbuckling figure who had ignited the imaginations of a weary populace, had left $992.50 in assets and $8,206 in debts.

If the Untouchables had investigated Eliot Ness in their usual manner, they would have discovered he was an honest cop.

# V.
# CLEVELAND'S BLACK EDISON

## Garrett Morgan invented the gas mask and automatic traffic signal but fought a lifetime for recognition

On July 25, 1916, with Cleveland in the midst of a heat wave intense enough to kill babies and prompt suicides, a ringing telephone broke the early morning stillness.

"Garrett Morgan?" an urgent voice asked.

"Yes," Morgan answered numbly.

"The same guy who invented some gas masks that are supposed to protect you from smoke?"

"The same. Who's this?"

"I'm from the city's safety department. There's been an explosion out on Number 5 crib and a lot of men are buried down there. We tried to get 'em but there's still some gas in the tunnel. We were wondering if you could bring out some of your gas masks."

"How do I get there?"

"Get down to the East Ninth pier. The George Wallace tug will be waiting for you."

Morgan grabbed an armful of gas masks, threw them in the back of his car, woke his brother Frank who lived next door and another neighbor, W.M. Roots, and was soon racing through the empty city streets at 50 m.p.h.—still barefoot and in his pajamas.

Later the three men stepped onto the crib where about 80 men — "sandhogs" — had been living while digging a 10-foot-wide tunnel, over 100 feet beneath Lake Erie's sandy bottom, to connect with the Division Avenue filtration plant. Cleveland, having long since outgrown the town well on Public Square, was expanding its system of water intake tunnels.

The second shift had been almost over when the sandhogs had hit a pocket of natural gas. (It wasn't the first such disaster: As a precaution, caged canaries were hung in the tunnel to warn of gas seepage.) There had been a spark—maybe from the electric lights or a pick hiting flint, no one would ever know for sure—and then the blast.

*Garrett Morgan proudly displaying the gold and diamond-studded bravery medal he recieved from a citizens committee for his rescue work at a mine explosion.*

*A young Garrett Morgan with wife Mary and sons (left to right) Garrett Jr., Cosmo and John.*

Two rescue parties had already gone into the tunnel but neither had returned. There was no telling how many men were trapped below.

Morgan called for volunteers to join him in another descent. No one moved. After a few seconds Frank, who fully understood his brother's invention, stepped forward. They were joined by Thomas Clancy, whose father-in-law had led one of the previous rescue parties, and one Thomas Castleberry of Rummersfield, Pennsylvania.

As Morgan donned the four-pound rubber and canvas mask and boarded the tunnel elevator, trailing long hoses behind him, Mayor Harry Davis shook his hand and wished him luck.

Morgan later recalled what happened at the bottom of the shaft in a 1966 *Plain Dealer* article.

"There was a door into the tunnel but I couldn't get it open. I could hear people pounding behind the door. The door had a glass in it, so I smashed the glass and I could hear the gas and compressed air whistle out. Then I could open the door because the pressure was off of it."

Still barefoot, he led the way into the dark tunnel past twisted rails, broken ties and hanging wires until the rescue party stumbled over the first body. Clancy produced an electric lantern. The man was dead. As others carried the body back to the elevator, Morgan's small band moved further into the tunnel. Morgan stepped on a live wire, igniting a spark, but nothing happened. The danger was past. Then they found Gus Van Deusen, Clancy's father-in-law and superintendent of the project, still breathing and rushed him back to the surface where they were met with a great cheer. Mayor Davis personally congratulated Morgan.

While Clancy stayed with his father-in-law new volunteers joined Morgan in two more expeditions into the tunnel. On one, he found Henry McNamara still alive and laid him across a cart of dead bodies, which the group then pulled back to the elevator. Morgan would have gone down a third time but officials from the U.S. Bureau of Mines arrived and put a stop to the rescue efforts. In all Morgan had brought out six of the bodies of 21 men who had died in the worst of Cleveland's six water-tunnel disasters, as well as the only two men who lived.

Feeling a little nauseous after his ordeal, Morgan returned home for some much-needed rest. When he awoke he hurriedly scanned the newspapers for the story of his heroic efforts. He should have known better. For although all four Cleveland dailies had dedicated their front pages almost exclusively to the tunnel disaster, only the *News* (in a single sentence) acknowledged that "G.A. and F.F. Morgan, negroes, led the third rescue party," the one that had saved Van Deusen's life. The others—the *Press, The Plain Dealer* and the *Leader*— simply mentioned that the brothers had been part of the rescue operations.

Garett Augustus Morgan was born on March 4, 1877, in Claysville, Kentucky, the second child of Sydney and Eliza Reed Morgan. Sydney Morgan

was the son of Confederate Colonel John Hunt Morgan, famed for leading Morgan's Raiders on a daring foray through Ohio, and his black mistress. Born in slavery, Sydney had been freed upon his father's death at the hands of Union soldiers.

Eliza Reed Morgan was the daughter of the Reverend Garrett Reed, who was the minister of Claysville, a small black section of Paris, Kentucky. Paris was a switch station on the railroad between Ohio and the Deep South and Sydney suffered through Reconstruction share-cropping and working on the Louisville and Nashville Railroad.

Garrett spent his youth helping out his minister grandfather, who lived across the street. The church of the day was the glue that held the community together, and Garrett's mother sang at the revival meetings that attracted the many blacks passing through Paris in search of a new life after slavery. Garrett's formal education ended in the sixth grade but he gained street savvy helping out on the Reverend Reed's horse and wagon, which was used by the community for general hauling as well as funerals.

At the age of 16 Garrett decided to set off on his own for Ohio, the state that had elected in 1855 the nation's first black public official (John Mercer Langston, clerk of Brownhelm Township). He found a job as a handyman for a rich landowner in Cincinnati and, after learning a number of trades that would later prove useful, he decided to try his luck in Cleveland, one of the few areas in the country where the abolitionist tradition still lingered, although ever so slightly. By the turn of the century most of the nation had turned its back on the plight of blacks. As Morgan told an American Missionary Association Convention in 1907, Cleveland gives the squarest deal of any town I ever lived in, but even here there is the same bar when it comes to employment. "We don't employ niggers here is what I got over and over after I was ready to do first-class work."

He arrived in Cleveland with one dime in his pocket and slept in boxcars in the Flats until he found a $5-a-week job sweeping floors at Roots and McBride, a dry goods store. From there he moved on to the H. Black Company (a large ladies' and children's clothes manufacturer that had originated the idea of standard sizes) and then to the L.M. Gross Company (another ladies garment manufacturer). His new work gave him the opportunity to display his inventive talents. Whenever a sewing machine broke down, he would fix it and it wasn't long before he became the only black machine adjuster in the city. His invention of accessories like a belt fastener that increased the machines' efficiency brought him to the attention of the latter company's founder, Louis N. Gross. Gross' son, William V., recalled that Morgan would come home with his father to work on ideas like a perpetual motion machine and a bath drain that would filter away scum without draining any water.

It was while working at Gross' that Morgan fell

# A better protection for the pedestrian, school children and R.R. crossing

An ad for Morgan's automatic traffic signal describing its safety advantages. The third position "shows traffic stopped in all directions, allowing the pedestrians to cross without fear of being struck by automobiles."

in love with Mary Hasek, a white Bohemian seamstress whose father had been a personal bodyguard for Austrian Emperor Franz Joseph. Because a new foreman took a dim view of Morgan's skin color and his relationship with Mary Hasek, Morgan soon decided to quit, vowing never to work for anyone again.

In 1907 he opened a sewing machine repair shop on West Sixth Street and the following year married Miss Hasek despite the shock waves generated in both families. (Although her parents eventually accepted the union, her brothers, with one exception, never did and asked Morgan not to attend their father's funeral, an incident which embittered him even more than the tunnel disaster.) His spouse's business acumen proved a valuable asset and he soon became one of the city's pioneer black businessmen, opening a 32-employe clothing manufacturing shop in his new home at 5202 Harlem Avenue, an all-white neighborhood in the heart of Cleveland's garment district.

One day Morgan was experimenting with a solution he had developed for use on the needle of a powerful sewing machine to prevent it from scorching cloth when a call to dinner interrupted him. He wiped his hands on a wiry cloth and went to eat. After dinner he noticed that the solution had straightened the wires of the cloth. So he experimented further with it on his Airedale, Towser, whose wiry hair also was straightened. After having proved the solution's safety on his own hair, Morgan organized the Garrett Morgan Hair Refining Company, which offered a full range of hair grooming products, in another section of his house.

The success of his new business guaranteed Morgan a steady income that allowed him to pursue other interests, most notably the gas mask. In 1912, he filed for a patent for it and talked a number of prominent white businessmen into forming the National Safety Device Company to produce and distribute it. Two years later he traveled to New Orleans to demonstrate his invention to the National Association of Fire Chiefs. To avoid prejudicing the case, former Cleveland Parks Director Charles P. Salen conducted the demonstration in which Morgan, disguised as "Big Chief Mason, a full-blood Indian from the Walpole Reservation in Canada," walked into a canvas tent filled with burning tar, sulphur and manure and emerged 20 minutes later, thanks to his gas mask, "as good as new." Morgan's invention won an award from the fire chiefs but he had to watch from the audience as Salen accepted it for him. That year he also won first grand prize for "the simplest and best life-saving device" at New York City's International Exposition of Safety and Sanitation.

Despite these awards, Morgan was relatively unknown in his hometown until the tunnel disaster of 1916. Even after the disaster he traveled a long rough road before finally gaining recognition. Thomas Clancy, the project superintendent's son-in-law, was made the popular hero of the rescue operation by the press and won a $500 Carnegie Hero Award. Morgan wasn't even asked to testify at the subsequent investigation of the disaster.

The injustice, however, did not go completely unnoticed. The Cleveland Chapter of the Association of Colored Men (forerunner to the NAACP) gave Morgan their own award, and a group of prominent white citizens led by Victor Sincere (general manager of Bailey's Department Store, a member of the Cleveland Chamber of Commerce and an officer and stockholder in Morgan's Safety Device Company) presented him with a diamond-studded medal that rivaled the Carnegie Hero Award.

Although the thought was important, the awards were little compensation to a proud man who would be haunted by tunnel-scene nightmares for the rest of his life. Many years later, after Morgan's continued campaign for justice became a story itself, the papers (led by Louis Seltzer's *Cleveland Press*) finally acknowledged his role in the rescue. But the incident "broke his heart in a way," his son, Garrett Jr., recalled.

By the 1920s Morgan had three young sons to take his mind off the tunnel disaster. He turned his attention to an invention he began work on after witnessing an accident between a horse-drawn wagon and an automobile: the traffic signal. At that time the automobile was still a novelty but an increasingly popular one which made necessary the manning of all major intersections by traffic cops holding semaphores. To protect pedestrians, who were fair game in the congested city streets (there were 120,000 cars in Cleveland by 1923), Morgan developed a folding electric traffic signal.

After testing his invention at the intersection of Vine and Erie Streets in Willoughby, Morgan sold the patent to General Electric for $40,000 in 1923. By April Fool's Day two years later, G.E. had installed a string of automatic lights along Euclid Avenue, which were controlled by a man in a signal tower at the East Ninth Street intersection. Fred Caley, secretary of Cleveland's Auto Club, declared that Morgan's invention "marked an epoch in Cleveland's metropolitan development," even though the confused citizenry couldn't figure out what the hell the yellow light was all about. But once again the newspapers, while cheering the fact the new light saved four minutes traveling time from Public Square to East 18th Street, made no mention of Morgan's contribution.

Morgan, however, was having too good a time with his new-found wealth to be disturbed by another slight. Besides playing a bit part in a Bert Williams movie, he bought a bus the size of a Pullman car and equipped it with a Pierce-Arrow engine, a White transmission, a Dodge hood, three bunks, a stove and an organ for his eldest son, John P., to play. When they pulled into small southern towns to hawk Morgan's hair products, the towns-people "looked at us like we were a bunch of freaks," John P. recalled. When the entourage was harassed by police, "Chief Morgan" simply pulled out his awards and medals from New Orleans, New York and Cleveland and went on his way.

Morgan's love for the outdoors (a holdover from his Kentucky childhood) led him to buy 160 acres of land along the Vermilion River so that Cleveland blacks could spend a weekend in the country. After work on Thursdays he would round up his family and employes (who were paid $75 a week when $30 was considered a good wage) and head out to his Wakeman Country Club, a recreational facility that included a hotel made from a barn, a baseball diamond that hosted black semi-pro teams and a boxing ring that doubled as a training camp for fighters.

In order to help sell his hair products he started a black newspaper, the *Cleveland Call*, but he ran into difficulty attracting black investors so he allowed others to buy stocks on the basis of their signature alone and put up the money himself. His generous spirit (he helped out black college students in many ways, including, as Judge Perry Jackson recalled, allowing Western Reserve's Alpha Phi Alpha fraternity to use his Harlem Avenue factory for initiation rites) led to his financial demise when the Depression hit.

The quiet inventor who, as local black historian Ichabod Flewellen remembered, "liked to withdraw to a corner and work on things," was more concerned with his inventions than his business affairs. He let others run his newspaper for him and after debts piled up because of unpaid advertising, he finally sold it to Edward Murrell's Pioneer Publishing Company, the printer of his hair product's labels. (The newspaper later merged with the *Post* to form today's Cleveland *Call and Post*.) Meanwhile his Wakeman Country Club was having difficulty attracting members because harassment from the local Ku Klux Klan (who went so far as to burn crosses on the club's lawn) forced members to carry rifles with them for protection.

This double drain on his finances, combined with the shattering effects of the Depression, was so discouraging that in 1934, shortly after the death of his brother Frank, he asked the city for a public grave, which they granted him as compensation for his rescue efforts. Morgan somehow weathered the Depression and settled into a peaceful retirement marred only by his gradual loss of sight from glaucoma. He still enjoyed toying with new ideas, such as a water capsule that would put out cigarettes automatically, and taking an occasional trip. Karen Gatewood recalls reading her grandfather biographies of other inventors and traveling with Morgan and his other grandchildren to the home of his lifelong idol, Thomas Edison. (Morgan's own home is still standing on Harlem Avenue.)

Then in 1963 it looked as if Morgan would finally fulfill a lifelong yearning for recognition when a black exposition in Chicago planned to include an exhibit of his accomplishments. But just as he was assembling material for the display, Garrett Morgan died.

As is so often the case in the lives of men, the nod of recognition he waited vainly for throughout his life came soon after his death on a rising tide of new black consciousness. In 1967 Cleveland Mayor Ralph Locher dedicated a plaque to Morgan that hangs in Cleveland Public Auditorium.

In 1974 his hometown in Kentucky changed its name to Garrett Morgan Place. And on July 24th, 1991, the 75th anniversary of Morgan's heroic rescue, the newly renovated Division Avenue Filtration Plant was re-named the Garrett Morgan Waterworks.

America has finally noticed Garrett Morgan.

# VI.
# LEAGUE PARK
## "There wasn't a bad seat in the house"

On May 1, 1891, twenty-five year old Denton Tecumseh "Cy" (for Cyclone) Young stood in the pitcher's box 55 feet from home plate, spit on a brand new Spalding baseball, smiled grimly, wound up his massive body and let loose the blazing fast ball that would make him baseball's winningest pitcher.

The Cincinnati Redlegs' "Biddy" McPhee didn't move a muscle in his blue flannel uniform as the ball shot into Charles "Chief" Zimmer's fingerless glove.

Umpire Phil Powers muttered "strike one" and League Park, the bright new red brick home of the Cleveland Spiders, began its illustrious career as the city's sports mecca.

By the time the Spiders won an easy 12-3 victory the record crowd of over 9000 fans were already in love with their new ballpark.

Professional baseball had come a long way in Cleveland since the first game in 1869 when the Cincinnati Red Stockings beat the Forest City's 25-6 and 2000 fans paid 25 cents to stand behind ropes at Case Commons (East 38th between Central and Community College Avenues).

The Spiders' old park on East 39th and Payne had been destroyed by lightning the previous year during a game with the Chicago Colts. With his grandstand splintered to bits Spider owner Frank DeHaas Robinson, also owner of the Payne and Superior streetcar lines, began searching for a field large enough to support the growing interest in the sport as well as make some money for his trolley line.

He found an open area at East 66th and Lexington Avenue and built a park where his streetcars could drop fans off 20 feet from the entrance.

Opening day marked the official beginning of summer in those days gone by. The fans, hungry for their first taste of the sport due to the May starting date, cheered the fourteen players (no coaches) of the 1891 Spiders as they paraded to the park in a decorated streetcar accompanied by balloons, circus animals and a 16 piece band.

*Cy Young still hurling at age 42.*

THE 1869 FOREST CITY'S, CLEVELAND'S FIRST PROFESSIONAL BASEBALL TEAM — Standing (left to right) are John Ward, left field; Eben Smith, shortstop and captain; Albert Pratt, pitcher; Arthur Burt, "middle field" and John Reiley, right field. Seated (left to right) are L.C. Hanna, second base; "Pickey" Smith, third base; Arthur Allison, first base and James "Deacon" White. Only White, Pratt, Allison, Ward and Reiley received salaries, White $125 a month and the rest $65 a month. There was no regular schedule and the average age of the players was 24 years old.

Ladies were admitted free to the grandstand every day except Saturdays and holidays (Sunday baseball was illegal in Ohio) and the starting line-up was introduced by an iron-lunged announcer standing behind home plate with a megaphone.

Pitchers were expected to finish the games they started, the gloves were the same size as the players' hands and the bunt, hit-and-run, squeeze and double steal were so new some managers were protesting that it was no longer baseball but a new game outside the rules.

The umpire (there was only one, usually an over-the-hill player) stood behind the pitcher until there were two strikes on the batter. He took more than his share of spiked toes and tobacco spit.

When the umpire turned his back runners often took a shortcut from first to third base without touching second. Sometimes the games ended in riots or teams walked off the field in protest.

Yet no one minded because League Park had an intimacy all its own. "There wasn't a bad seat in the house," the old timers will tell you. The fans sat on wooden benches so close to the field they could watch the players sweat and hear them cuss.

The park's good vibrations seemed to inspire the Spiders, already one of the rowdiest teams in the league under player-manager Pat Tebeau. In 1892 the National League expanded to 12 teams so the season was split into a spring and fall season with a playoff set for the end of the season.

Cleveland won the second half thanks to a highly successful home stand and earned a shot at first half champ the Boston Beaneaters.

As 6,000 fans flocked to League Park to watch the opening contest the press dubbed the best-of-nine playoff "The World Series."

Cy Young and Happy Jack Stivett dueled for 11 scoreless innings before the game was finally called because of darkness. It turned out to be the Spiders' best effort as the superior Beaneaters won the next five straight games to become the champs.

The following year there was an attempt to put more slugging in the game by replacing the pitcher's box with a rubber slab and moving it 60 feet six inches from the home plate. (The six inches was a surveyor's error in reading his instructions but has stuck ever since.)

While the pitchers were adjusting their curves,

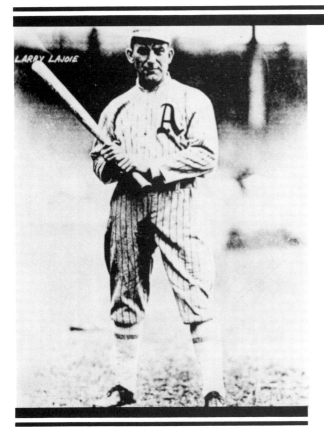

*Napoleon "Larry" Lajoie, namesake of the Naps.*

screwballs and sinkers the batters were having a field day. Left fielder Jesse Burkett's bat (.423 in '95 and .410 in '96) kept the Spiders in the Temple Cup playoffs that replaced the split season. But despite their success attendance dwindled.

So in the winter of 1898 Robinson bought the St. Louise franchise and shuttled off most of the Spiders' stars, including Young and Burkett. Cleveland fans wasted little time in venting their anger, labelling what was left of the team "The Misfits."

The fans boycotted League Park so successfully that before the season ended it became a ghost park with the Spiders playing all their games on the road. They finished 80 games out of first and their record of 20 victories and 134 defeats, the worst in baseball history, marked the end of the Spiders.

League Park remained abandoned until the turn of the century when Ban Johnson's Western League changed its name to the American and threatened a full scale attack on the National League's players. In order to avoid a confrontration directors of both leagues met at Cleveland's Hollenden Hotel where Johnson agreed to retain minor league status for another year.

As part of the deal Jack Kilfoyl, owner of a men's furnishing store on public square, and Charley Somers, who inherited his father's rich coal business, were allowed to purchase the Western League's Grand Rapids franchise, move it to Cleveland and lease League Park off Robinson.

Somers, "the father of the American League," used his wealth to keep the infant league alive in its first few years. He lent Charley Comiskey enough to build a park in Chicago while saving franchises in Philadelphia, St. Louis and Boston.

Cleveland's new team was known as the Blues because they used the Spiders' old uniforms. They finished seventh their first year in the American League and the city took a cool view of them, considering them inferior to the National League.

By 1902 the Broncos (they'd changed their name again) were so hard up for pitchers manager Bill Armour held an open tryout at League Park. After watching semi-pro Otto Hess throw for awhile he used him against the Washington Senators the same afternoon.

Hess won 7-6 in 10 innings and went on to become a 20 game winner.

The next day the Philadelphia Athletics were in town and once again Armour didn't know who to pitch. He confessed his dilemma to ticket-taker Herman Schleman, who pointed out Charley Smith of the Cleveland Wheel Club sitting out in the bleachers. Armour told him to put on a uniform and Smith, who came to League Park to watch a game, won one by beating the A's 5-4.

That same year the A's Connie Mack, one of the game's all-time great managers, repaid Somers for saving his franchise by selling him Napoleon Lajoie, his star second baseman. Mack had stolen Lajoie from his hometown rivals, the Phillies, the year before but had to release him to avoid a legal battle. Lajoie was such an asset that within two years he was managing the team that had been renamed the Naps in his honor.

During the Lajoie era League Park enjoyed some if its finest moments, including pitcher Addie Joss' perfect game (the fourth in the sport's history) against the Chicago White Sox in the heat of the 1908 pennant race.

Lajoie created such an interest in the team that by 1909 the owners expanded the park. Fred Ritz, who saw his first game in 1901 while attending Dunham School across the street from the right field fence, remembered the expansion gobbling up four houses to the east of the field.

Since the park's other three sides were also boxed in by rows of houses there was nowhere else to add seats but up, which guaranteed the fans would continue to have a good view once a second level was completed.

The wooden grandstands and pavillion were replaced by a steel and concrete base to avoid the fires which were plaguing other parks around the country. Individual box seats became available for the first time but wooden benches remained in the general admission and newly constructed left field bleachers.

Like most other parks in its era League Park has a distinct personality which influenced the makeup of the home team the way Boston's

New Base Ball Park, Cleveland, Ohio.          24259

*League Park, East 66th and Lexington Avenue, as displayed on a penny post card circa 1910. Paddy Livingston (left), Cleveland sandlot star who caught in the 1911 League Park All-Star game as a member of the World Champion Philadelphia Athletics, and George Uhle, Babe Ruth's arch-nemesis*

Fenway Park still does today.

While right-handed hitters had an almost impossible home run shot to left field, 375 feet down the line and 460 feet in center, lefties merely had to pull a fly 290 feet down the right field line to clear the fence stretching along Lexington Avenue.

It wasn't very long before even the right-handers began punching the ball to the right.

"It was a left-handed park, one of the greatest in the country for the fans," George Uhle, a Cleveland pitcher in the 1920's, remembered. "You'd try to throw your best stuff away from them."

"The dark scoreboard and no fans in center field made a good background for the hitters but I liked to pitch there anyway," he continued. "Most pitchers were afraid to let up on the great hitters like Ruth, Gehrig and Cobb but I was a slow-baller and it was the best park to let up in. They could hit anyone's fast ball over the fence, even if you threw it under the plate."

During the expansion they replaced the wooden fence, complete with knotholes that magically reappeared each time the management filled them in, with 20 feet of concrete and 20 feet of wire screen.

The new wall, however, wreaked havoc on the right fielder's sensibilities. While the left and center fielders had enough room to make stunning over the shoulder catches, robbing hitters of inside-the-park home runs, the right fielder had to make a split-second decision on each hit.

He might chase a liner up to the wall only to have it land above his head and be retrieved by the second baseman. Or he might stand back waiting to catch it off the wall only to discover it was low enough to be caught in the first place. Or it might hit one of the steel beams protruding out from the concrete and bounce over to left field.

If it hit the screen above, perhaps catching a rising liner that would be a home run in another park, it usually rebounded honestly. But then again it might get stuck in the screen or drop as if dead.

Anything fielded cleanly off the wall meant a close play at second base. More often than not the runner would be thrown out. The fans quickly discovered that any hit to right field with its wall of surprises was sure to generate an exciting play. Kids began to play "wall" by the hour, having a friend lob flies against the side of a garage.

As the kids grew up they brought their friends along, creating larger and larger crowds. For the next three decades "Take Me Out To The Ball Park" became something of a national anthem.

An excursion to cozy League Park on a summer afternoon was like a family picnic. The gates opened around noon for the 3:30 game so the fans could watch batting practice. The many school kids who received free tickets were usually the first to arrive.

Dan Keegan, the Indians' 1920 bat boy, lived right behind the ball park. "No kid ever thought of paying," he recalled. A large group would always gather on Lexington Avenue eyeballing the skyline for a hit coming over the screen. If they returned the ball it was good for a free admission.

Others laid on their stomachs by the crack beneath the exit gate in the wall, hollering at the outfielders during batting practice to throw a few more over. They often obliged.

Some kids worked their way inside by selling concessions. Bob Gill, who began checking out the vendors' white coats as a 13 year old in 1933 and retired as the Indians' travelling secretary, remembered selling peanuts, popcorn, cracker jack, hot dogs and Parfay, a bottled drink for a dime.

Once the men inside the scoreboard, which did not acknowledge the existence of the National League, began posting the players' numbers instead of their names, kids would line up in front of the printing office under the stands to pick up scorecards. Although fans complained that for the price of a five cent scorecard you could buy a good cigar, they were placated by a free pair of tickets if their scorecard had the lucky number.

One time the printing office made a mistake and the entire crowd won. The scoreboard also kept an inning by inning report of the other American League games.

Nick and Mike Kackloudis also grew up in the neighborhood. They remembered the kids who didn't make it inside the park climbing the fire escape at Dunham School across the street, even though it only offered a partial view of the field.

The best view was from the top of the Andrews Storage company but that required a much more dangerous climb. Indians' groundskeeper Harold Bossard recalled that the club had to replace 20-30 broken windows a year in the surrounding buildings from long home run balls.

As the kids were trying every trick imaginable to sneak into the park, the dressed-up downtown businessmen, high-fashioned ladies and factory workers who conveniently became sick at lunchtime began arriving on streetcars, bicycles, horse and buggies and even a few automobiles. At first local residents were honored if a car parked near their house but as their popularity grew they'd park three or four autos on their lawn for a quarter apiece.

Inside the park the newspaper reporters dodged foul tips in the windowless press box which hung right over home plate. Next to them sat Jack Graney, the ex-player radio announcer who was so good he could recreate away games off a ticker tape in his Cleveland studio without his listeners guessing otherwise.

Graney would conveniently work in his sponsor's products with phrases like "the center fielder's riding the Red Wing (Mobil gasoline's trademark) back for the fly ball, he's got it!"

Meanwhile the players down on the field entertained the fans during warm-ups with spirited games of pepper a la the Harlem Globetrotters.

**TRIS SPEAKER**

Born at Hubbard, Texas, April 4, 1888.
Weight 180 lbs.        Height 5:11½.
Bats left.        Throws left.
Joined Cleveland Club April 12, 1916.

As the pitchers ran laps and shagged flies other players chatted with the fans hanging over the stands.

In those days players weren't traded like baseball cards. Most of them lived in the town they played and they stuck around long enough for the fans to know their backgrounds like one of the family.

During a game the fans sat close enough to hurl a personal insult if the player messed up but afterwards they'd share a few fishbowls at one of the neighborhod cafes before heading home to dinner.

Professional baseball was more like a steady job before night games, jet air travel and hectic scheduling made the players strangers to each other as well as the fans.

One example of the closeness which developed among the players during the many long train rides was the Addie Joss benefit, baseball's first all-star type game.

On July 24, 1911 a collection of what the *Cleveland Plain Dealer* called THE GREATEST ARRAY OF PLAYERS EVER SEEN ON ONE FIELD converged on League Park for a game against the Naps.

Paddy Livingston, a spitball catcher who learned the art on Cleveland's sandlots but was playing for the World Champion Philadelphia Athletics at the time, caught for the All Stars.

For 25 cents to $1 the fans watched Ty Cobb, Tris Speaker, Eddie Collins, Sam "Home Run" Baker and Walter Johnson defeat the Naps 5-3 and raise $13,000 for the deceased Joss' family.

In 1914 Lajoie was released after finishing in the cellar for the first time. In his absence the team was renamed the Indians to honor Louis Sockalexis, a slugging Penobscot outfielder who starred on the '97 Spiders.

A committee of sports writers who chose the name believed Sockalexis was the first American Indian to play in the majors. (Actually, it was James Toy of Cleveland's 1887 American Association Team.)

Two years after Lajoie's departure James Dunn, the club's new owner, purchased Tris Speaker, Boston's superstar center fielder, for $55,000 and two players, the sport's largest deal at the time.

By 1920 "The Grey Eagle" (Speaker's nickname because of prematurely greying temples) molded the strange collection of waiver price castoffs and minor league acquisitions into the city's first American League pennant winner.

In the final days of the season, however, the second place Chicago White Sox were exposed for throwing the 1919 World Series. League President Ban Johnson claimed they had also been pressured by the same gamblers to let the Indians win the pennant.

Besides causing a crackdown on pre-game re-

*THE 1920 WORLD CHAMPION CLEVELAND INDIANS — Player-manager Tris Speaker (center, seated) is flanked by team owner James Dunn (left) and secretary Walter McNichols. Next to McNichols is Elmer "Grand Slam" Smith and pitching star Stanley Coveleski. "Triple Play" Bill Wamby is third from the right in the top row. The team wore black arm bands in memory of shortstop Ray Chapman (upper corner insert), major league baseball's only fatality, who was struck by a Carl Mays submarine fastball in mid-season.*

*Bob Feller as a teenage flame thrower at League Park.*

lations between the players and fans, the scandal took the sweetness out of Cleveland's long awaited championship. The best-of-nine World Series was the team's last hope for vindication.

After losing two and winning one against the Brooklyn Trolley Dodgers in New York, the series shifted to Cleveland where pitcher Stanley Coveleski won his second game to even it up.

On a bright Sunday afternoon 26,684 fans jammed Dunn Field (re-named by the owner after winning the pennant) to watch Jim "Sarge" Bagby (31-12) face Brooklyn's spitball artist Burleigh Grimes.

George Uhle, the tribe's young hurler at the time, recalled that first baseman George Burns noticed that Brooklyn's second baseman tipped off Grimes' spitter by shifting the dirt in his hands before the pitch in case he had to handle the wet ball.

Armed with that information Cleveland left fielder Charley Jamieson opened the first inning with a line drive off the first baseman's glove that rolled into the standing room crowd roped along the wall. Bill Wamby hit a ground single between short and third and Speaker surprised the Dodgers with a bunt to fill the bases.

Elmer Smith stepped up to the plate, fouled off the first pitch, looked at a ball and a strike, and then smacked the next pitch over the screen in right field for the first grand slam home run in a World Series game.

The fans went wild, showering the field with papers and cushions, but there was more to come.

In the fifth inning, with the Dodgers' Pete Kilduff on second and Otto Miller on first, second baseman Wamby leaped high in the air to stab a Clarence Mitchell liner, stepped on second to double Kilduff and turned toward first to find the amazed Miller standing only a few short feet away.

Wamby easily tagged the Dodger catcher for the first and only unassisted triple play in World Series history. The crowd, not understanding what happened until the Indians began to run off the field, went berserk once again.

It was League Park's finest hour.

The Indians won the next two games for four straight home victories and a World Championship without a trace of the scandal that marred the 1919 Series.

Although League Park continued to entertain in the holiday spirit the rest of the decade was dominated by Babe Ruth's New York Yankees. Pitcher George Uhle, Ruth's personal nemesis, seemed to have a knack for striking out the mighty Babe with slow curves around the belly or knee.

Uhle claimed the hardest hit ball he ever saw at League Park was Ruth's line shot that was still going up when it hit the top of the screen near the scoreboard in center field (460 feet). "It was the most terrific hit I ever saw," Uhle recalled. "It would've landed on East 79th street but the screen stopped it and he only got a double."

In 1929 Ruth hit his 500th home run over the right field wall and gave Jack Geiser, the kid who returned the ball, a $20 bill, an autographed baseball and a chance to sit in the Yankee dugout.

That same year construction began on a new Lakefront Municipal Stadium that could hold three times as many spectators as League Park. But instead of "the wall" it had an outfield of such dimensions (before the fences were added) that Babe Ruth cracked, "You'd have to have a horse to play outfield there."

After the 1933 Indians played 77 games in their cavernous new stadium their batting average dropped to seventh in the league. The following year they retreated to the comfortable confines of old League Park except on Sundays and holidays. The move cut the stadium rental costs to help offset the effects of the depression and improved the team's batting average.

But League Park's days were numbered. Even the appearance of Bob Feller, a high school kid from Iowa who struck out 17 Philadelphia Athletics to tie Dizzy Dean's record his first year in the park, was not enough to turn the clock back. Its wooden superstructure was deteriorating and a violent windstorm blew down part of the wall.

On June 22, 1946 Bill Veeck, the open-collared fun-loving promoter who would turn Cleveland into a baseball madhouse, bought the club for $1.6 million.

Instead of retreating to his offices after closing the deal, Veeck limped into the bleachers on a leg injured in World War II. "Welcome to Cleveland, Mr. Veeck," a grizzled fan greeted the already familiar curly top. "Just call me Bill," Veeck responded as he made himself comfortable among the 50 cent boys.

A new era was dawning in Cleveland baseball and Veeck with his orchestras, circuses, free days and other promotions (including a pennant winning team) needed room to seat the over two million fans who would flock to see the tribe in 1948.

Before he left, however, he noticed another phenomenon at League Park on the Sundays when the Indians played out of town: black baseball.

The Cleveland Buckeyes were the city's representative in the American Negro League since 1942 and as far back as 1931 black fans stuffed the park to watch Satchel Paige pitch for the Cleveland Cubs against such barnstorming stars as Josh Gibson, the Homestead Gray's legendary catcher who hit over 800 home runs in his career.

Alonzo Boone, who pitched for both the Cubs and the Buckeyes, remembered Gibson hitting a home run over a laundry on Lexington Avenue, quite a feat for a right-handed hitter.

The Buckeyes brought attention to the quality of the Negro League by dethroning the Gray's as World Series champs in 1945, winning one game before over 10,000 fans at League Park.

Veeck, who was unable to resist such an untapped source of spectators, signed Larry Doby as the American League's first black baseball player in

*Cleveland Buckeye pitchers Gene Bremmer (left), who won the second game of the 1945 Negro World Series, and Alonzo Boone, who later managed the club.*

*THE 1946 CLEVELAND BUCKEYES — American Negro League Champs in 1945 and 1947, the 1946 team featured center-fielded Sam Jethroe (fifth from the left in the top row) who later played in the National League for the Boston Braves.*

1947, the same year he took the Indians out of League Park forever.

With its baseball team gone the old park was left with only one professional sports function, practice field for the fledging Cleveland Browns of the All-American Football Conference.

Although League Park was built for baseball, "the national pastime," down through the years it had also hosted the city's first pro football team, the Cleveland Bulldogs, the nationally respected Big Four college teams (Western Reserve, Case Tech, John Carroll and Baldwin Wallace) and the "News Skippies," a 16 and under team sponsored by the Cleveland News.

Sports Editor Ed Bang, dean of the nation's sports writers, organized the team to raise money for the kids during the depression. In those days there were few practices (because even the pros held other jobs), little equipment and few fans.

On November 11, 1945, however, the previously mediocre Cleveland Rams, tied with Detroit for first place in the National Football League's Western Division, hosted the defending champion Green Bay Packers before 28,686 League Park stalwarts.

Ram halfback Fred Gehrke raced 42 and 72 yards for a pair of scores, the Packers Irv Comp hit Clyde Goodnight on a 75 yard touchdown pass and Rams quarterback Bob Waterfield threw an 84 yard scoring toss to end Jim Benton, all in the first quarter.

In the excitement the fans hardly noticed that the temporary stands, the first ones ever put up for a football game, collapsed near the end of the period.

As police and ambulances rushed to rescue the 700 fans who fell to the ground, the loudspeaker cautioned those nearby to vacate the area. Almost no one moved, fearing to miss some of the excitement.

Although the Rams went on to beat the Washington Redskins for the NFL title, owner Dan Reeves took his team to Los Angeles to make room for Paul Brown's new team, the Cleveland Browns.

Brown used League Park as a practice field where he experimented with his many innovations that would eventually revolutionize pro football.

The top of the Andrews Storage Company across the street soon found itself supporting unknown faces with binoculars instead of the familiar neighborhood kids.

The City of Cleveland, which bought League Park from the Indians, demolished all but one side of the park in 1951 when it turned the grounds into a playground.

For the next three decades the park slowly deteriorated until a new generation discovered the lost jewel. On August 25, 1979 the Lexington Avenue neighborhood joined the rest of the city in celebrating League Park Day, declaring the refurbished site a Cleveland Landmark. Further restoration is planned.

Today any kid can go out to League Park and hit a few baseballs where Ruth, Cobb, Speaker and Gibson once roamed. But they can't turn one in to watch them play.

# VII.
# WHEN EAGLES GATHERED
## The national air races, Cleveland's Kentucky Derby

Lieutenant James (Jimmy) Doolittle, one of America's pioneer aviators, was testing a safety device in his Army pursuit plane above Cleveland Hopkins airport when he noticed his wing ripping off.

Doolittle, who earned a hero's reputation testing instrument landing devices with a cover over his cockpit, calmly hit the silk, parachuting to safety as his plane crashed on a farm in Olmsted Falls.

As the story goes, Doolittle then walked back over to his Hopkins hanger and asked for another plane, adding another anecdote to his already growing legend.

The year was 1929 and airplane pilots were still regarded as devil-may-care rogues who risked their lives every time they left the ground.

Doolittle's escapade set the stage for what may be the most exciting extravaganza in Cleveland's history, the first National Air Races. The show would eventually draw attention to our city the way the Kentucky Derby does to Louisville and the Indianapolis 500 to the capital of Indiana.

Cleveland waited nine years to host the event.

The idea of an air show first came to America from Europe in 1920 when Ralph Pulitzer, publisher of the *New York World,* put up the money for a race on Long Island's Mitchell Field. Pulitzer wanted to reawaken interest in aviation, which was suffering from postwar apathy.

The show circulated to different cities each year and was finally brought to Cleveland by a group of local businessmen headed by Louis W. Greve and Frederick C. Crawford.

Greve was president of the Cleveland Pneumatic Tool Company, which made the hydraulic undercarriages that held the wheels on the planes. Crawford was general manager and later president of Thompson Products Inc., now a part of TRW Inc. Thompson Products developed the experimental sodium-cooled cylinders which enabled Charles Lindbergh's *Spirit of St. Louis* to reach France.

*"Smiling" Doug Davis with the first Thompson Trophy in 1929.*

Lt. James "Jimmy" Doolittle, 1932 Thompson Trophy winner.

"If the weather was bad you still had to pay your bills so we got the local hotels and merchants to underwrite the air show—like the Hotel Statler would promise in writing to pay $5000 if we needed it," explained Crawford. "They stood to make a lot of money if it came off."

Companies which made airplane parts were asked to offer cash prizes for the various races.

"I was a kid fresh out of high school and working for Captain James Inglefield, a friend of Jimmy Doolittle's," recalled Clay Herrick, a retired advertising executive and Cleveland historian. "Inglefield was a high-pressure telephone salesman who called the city's leading industrialists and talked them into buying a box of seats for their employees. Once they agreed, he would send me over to collect the money before they had a chance to change their minds."

The air show ran from August 24 through September 2, 1929. The Roaring Twenties were at their peak, the stock market was making millionaires out of shoe shine boys, and locally the Terminal Tower (hailed as "the tallest building in the world outside of New York City") was rising skyward on Public Square.

Cleveland, under City Manager W.R. Hopkins, prepared to throw the biggest party in its history.

The inauguration ceremonies opened with a downtown flower parade that put the Rose Bowl Tournament parade to shame. An estimated 300,000 spectators from all over the country watched 200 floats, 21 bands and 1,500 marchers strut down

Euclid Avenue as three Goodyear blimps flew overhead.

In conjunction with the air show, a three-million-dollar display of planes opened at Public Hall, 5,000 pigeons were released on Public Square, and aerial acrobatics and fireworks reigned overhead. Over 100,000 spectators jammed the country roads out to Hopkins Airport for the opening day of the races.

Hopkins (named after the city manager) opened four years earlier as "the first major municipal-owned airport in the world." Its one-square-mile area, well-lighted runways and level surface free from hazards made it an ideal location for such races.

The city built what would become a permanent grandstand, hangars were available for visiting aircraft and there was enough space left over for taking off and landing without interfering with airport operations.

For the next nine days Cleveland was the air capital of the world. And since in 1929 airplanes were still considered something of a science fiction fantasy, the exciting events here were reported in newspapers around the world.

From 1 p.m. to 6 p.m. daily there was enough action to rivet the attention of the most hardened newsman.

"Lucky" Lindbergh, America's hero of the 1920's, dove his plane in front of the grandstands on opening day, looped 200 feet off the ground, shut off his motor while upside down and landed out of his loop exactly in formation with the other Navy planes lined up on the runway.

Charles "Lucky" Lindbergh.

Amelia Earhart.

*Doug Davis' Travelair "Mystery Ship," winner of Cleveland's first National Air Races in 1929. Notables in attandance (from left to right) City Manager W.R. Hopkins, Anne Morrow Lindbergh, Air Races Manager Cliff Henderson, Charles Lindbergh, Wm. P. MacCracken, Assistant Secretary of Commerce for Aeronautics and Goodyear President P.W. Litchfield.*

Lindbergh performed daily with the Navy High Hats , the Blue Angels of their time, who tied the wings of their biplanes together with 35 feet of rope, took off, flew difficult maneuvers and landed without breaking the ropes.

As the spectators craned their necks skyward, other Army, Navy, Marine and civilian pilots provided plenty of thrills.

Lieutenant Al Williams, the U.S. Navy's speed king, did a complete circuit of the airport, flying upside down less than 200 feet above ground. He nearly gave the crowd heart failure by appearing to land upside down before flopping over at the last possible second.

Charles "Speed" Holman, operations manager for Northwestern Airways, tried to sell a skeptical public on the safety of commercial flying by doing loops and upside-down turns with a 14-passenger Ford Tri-Motor.

Spain's Juan de la Cierva gave the first American demonstration of his vertical ascending and landing "autogyro," an early version of the helicopter. The Navy's huge dirigible *Los Angeles* soared over the show, demonstrating for the first time "the sky hook," the transfer of a passenger from a plane to the blimp on a rope ladder.

Even *Graf Zeppelin*, the world's most famous dirigible, changed course on its historic around-the-world flight to pass over Cleveland on the way to its Lakehurst, New Jersey, dock. Dr. Hugo Eckener, the *Graf* commander, then returned to Cleveland as "guest of honor" on the last day of the show.

There were daily parachute jumping contests, glider demonstrations, Goodyear blimp flights, closed-course racing and cross-country races from as far away as Los Angeles, Miami and Toronto, all timed to reach Cleveland on different days of the show.

Women pilots, including the already famous Amelia Earhart, raced in a special "Powder Puff Derby" from Santa Monica, California, to Cleveland.

Yet it was the closed-course racing that provided the most thrills for the fans in the stands. The first "free-for-all" Thompson-sponsored race was 5 laps around a 10-mile circuit from the finish line in front of the grandstand to a pylon 10 miles out in the country.

"Smiling " Doug Davis, a civilian pilot from Atlanta, left America's two fastest military fighter planes blowing in the wind as his "mystery plane" passed the finish line at an average speed of 194.9 miles per hour.

"In those days a barnstormer could build a plane in his barn and beat the army," Crawford recalled. "They asked the army, 'What do you need planes for?' and they said they wanted little planes that could go out to sea 200 miles and look for an enemy fleet."

Davis's plane gained the "mystery" tag because he kept it covered with canvas until the day of the race, fearing other pilots would steal his design. Actually, there were no radical new designs in Davis's

*Scarlet Marvel*, only minute attention to streamling and weight reduction. It was the air show that provided the testing ground for such innovations.

Until World War II replaced the lonely pilot-inventor with rooms full of engineers, the National Air Races were the aviation industry's laboratory.

In 1930 the races were held in Chicago, but the National Aeronautical Association which licensed the races returned the show to Cleveland on the basis of its 1929 success. The Cleveland show had turned a profit of $90,000. The only other show city to ever more than break even was Spokane, Washington, in 1927. Spokane only made $485.

In the following years the Thompson Race became the standard, and the Thompson Trophy, based on the Greek legend of Icarus who melted his feathered wings by flying too close to the sun, became equal in stature to the Green Jacket of the Masters Golf Tournament. The top aviators in the world competed for the right to keep it for a year.

By 1931 the closed-course races and speed dashes had replaced most of the cross-country races. The Thompson Race first prize was increased to $7,500, a large sum during the Depression. But the danger element, just like that of the Indy 500, was what kept the crowds coming back.

Six pilots were killed in the 1929 event. All but one died during cross-country trips away from Hopkins Airport. Thomas Reid crashed in nearby Fairview Park trying to set a new solo endurance record.

It was not until 1934 that one of the closed-course racers went down. By that time the Depression had cut the purses, and the show had shrunk to a Labor Day weekend festival, similar to today's air show.

A capacity crowd watched in terror on Labor Day 1934 as Doug Davis, winner of the 1929 race, went straight up in the air in his Wedell-Williams #44, came back down in a spin and disappeared behind a clump of trees in North Olmsted.

It was later learned that Davis had cut inside a pylon, realized he had to circle back or lose the race, and whipped his plane in too tight a turn, causing the right wing to tear off.

Davis's death allowed Roscoe Turner, the flamboyant barnstormer, to win his first Thompson Race.

Turner returned the following year, losing the Bendix race from Los Angeles to Cleveland by 23 seconds to Benny Howard. It was the closest finish in the distance race's history. Turner vowed he'd be avenged in the Thompson Race which had been expanded to 10 laps around a 15-mile course.

Over 85,000 spectators, many from behind the fences, watched Turner keep the lead for eight laps. Then a supercharger blade on his big Hornet engine snapped off, leaving him with a split-second decision. Rather than bail out, lose his expensive plane and put the crowd in jeopardy, Turner landed the smoking plane with a couple bounces in front of the finish

*Frederick C. Crawford, president of Thompson Products Inc., presenting the Thompson Trophy to 1934 winner Roscoe Turner and his winning aircraft, the golden Wedell-Williams Special. The plane is currently on display at the Crawford Auto-Aviation Museum.*

line, stealing the show from the other planes.

As Turner pulled up in his disabled plane, Jack Story, the race's P.A. announcer, hollered, "Tough Luck, Roscoe."

"Say, that was the best luck I ever had in my life," Turner replied. "I'm lucky to be here at all."

Since the races continued to be a success despite the Depression, the National Aeronautical Association gave Cleveland a five-year option on the races. In 1936, however, an expansion project at Hopkins forced the races to move to Los Angeles.

"We took the whole show to the West Coast, along with Cleveland people and Cleveland money," Crawford recalled.

The Thompson Race returned to Cleveland the following year, and it proved to be the most exciting race ever, a regular David versus Goliath contest.

Earl Ortman's big black Bromberg Special was battling Roscoe Turner's plane neck and neck most of the race when Turner's oil-splashed windshield made him think he'd missed a pylon.

As Turner re-circled the pylon, falling behind, Ortman throttled back to save his engine, thinking he'd won.

However, Rudy Kling, an auto mechanic from Illinois, shot past Ortman in his light yellow Folkerts racer just as they crossed the finish line. It happened so fast that many of the spectators missed it. Kling himself thought he'd finished second, nicking Ortman by an amazingly close 256.910 miles per hour to 256.858 miles per hour.

In 1938 the aeronautical association announced rule changes in what was becoming known as the Cleveland Air Races. There would be only two high-speed events, the Thompson and Greve races, and qualifying races would decide the best starting positions. The Thompson Race was increased to 300 miles, 30 laps arouns a 10-mile course. A record pre-war purse of $45,000 would be shared, $18,000 going to the first-place plane.

Only eight planes qualified for what was billed as "300 miles of the world's toughest flying." Roscoe Turner was again the favorite, answering a pre-race rumor that the other fliers would try to box him in with a gruff, "Anyone who tries it will have his tail chewed off by my propeller."

He went on to win his second Thompson Trophy when Ortman missed a pylon.

As war clouds rose over Europe, it became increasingly difficult for the private fliers to gain the financial support necessary for the increasingly sophisticated planes.

Turner did it by selling himself. "He was a great flyer and showman," Crawford recalled. "A barnstormer, he made his money by advertising for people. For publicity he designed his own uniforms, real fancy with big belt buckles, wore a handlebar moustache and took a lion cub with him in a cab downtown. He was a great showman, made his name in the air races, and the kids loved him."

After Turner won for the third time in 1939

(allowing him to keep the trophy), he announced his retirement. It marked the end of an era.

There were no new plane designs emerging, and the military was withdrawing its support from the Air Show to concentrate on the war in Europe. As the U.S. geared up its war machine, the races were discontinued.

Over the years the highly publicized accidents and deaths associated with the races were often blamed for hampering the airplane's evolution as a legitimate means of transportation. But the races stimulated engine and structural innovation, which made America's air power the decisive factor in the Allies' war victory.

But in the early years, "it was peacetime and there was no Air Force, for the army controlled the airplanes and there were few appropriations for aviation," Crawford recalled. "Today the Air Force gives the Cleveland Air Races great credit for maintaining interest in aviation while the military did nothing. Congress was ready to vote money for aviation when the time came."

After the war the Aircraft Industrial Association, the trade group of aircraft manufacturers, wanted an East and West Coast show to display the advances made during the war. Cleveland and Los Angeles were chosen because they had the best facilities. And Cleveland obtained another five-year franchise from the aeronautical association to host the races.

Planes developed during the war years dwarfed the older aircraft but used fighter planes like Mustangs or P-51s were available for as low as $1,000.

A new jet division was added to include the latest Air Force weaponry. Large-scale military participation promised to show the taxpayers what they'd been paying for.

"In 1946 the public was reading about aviation during the war so we put on a helluva show," Crawford remembered. "We conceived an air foundation. A lot of aviation people put up over a quarter of a million dollars to underwrite the show. We had a budget of over $700,000, built new grandstands by the bomber plant as well as other facilities and still made a profit. We saved some to start the next year's show and gave the rest to charities like the Air Force Relief Fund for the families of pilots killed in action."

Ninety pilots from across the country modified their surplus planes for the races. Twenty-five entered the Thompson Race alone. Competition ran high after the seven year layoff, and the planes were required to pass strict safety and ability tests. Pilots were required to wear crash helmets and parachutes.

Six Lockheed P-80 jet airplanes, all with military pilots, gave the public its first glimpse of the jet age. Over 180,000 spectators paid for a close-up view of America's air might as Tex Johnson, a 32-year-old test pilot, won the reciprocating engine (propeller) division at a speed of 373.908 miles per hour, 90 miles per hour faster than Roscoe Turner's time in 1939.

For the next two years, Captain Cook Cleland,

*Firemen and residents cleaning up the debris from Bill Odom's fateful crash into a Berea home.*

# GLENN CURTISS' RECORD FLIGHT

Practically everyone who's made it through high school has heard of Charles Lindbergh's famous solo flight across the Atlantic Ocean. It was THE BIG EVENT of the Roaring 20's and made Lindbergh an instant hero to millions of Americans.

However, Lindbergh's flight and the enormous reaction to it obscured another solo flight that received almost as much attention in a less hectic decade.

On August 31, 1910 while aviation was still in its infancy, Glenn Curtiss, a quiet young man who would go on to head his own airplane company, set the world's over-the-water flight record on a trip from Euclid Beach Amusement Park in Cleveland to Cedar Point Park outside Sandusky.

An estimated half million people lined the shore of Lake Erie to witness the historic flight sponsored by the Cleveland Press. Both Euclid Beach and Cedar Point broke attendance records and the city of Sandusky declared a business holiday to welcome Curtiss. If anyone could keep his Hudson Flier aloft for the full 72 miles, Curtiss, the winner of the International Cup at Rheims, France the previous year, could.

"Probably no event of its kind was ever witnessed by more people, a vast concourse of the people of Northern Ohio having gathered on the shore of the Lake between both points," a souvenir program for the Cleveland Aviation Meet later the same year recapped the event. "It was one of the most successful and epoch-making flights in the history of aviation."

Curtiss accomplished his remarkable feat under the most difficult conditions. Not only were the air currents over Lake Erie considered treacherous a 29-year-old East Cleveland resident, former Thompson Products employee and World War II Navy flying ace, inherited Roscoe Turner's role as the man to beat.

Cleland fought through military red tape to purchase two Navy Corsair fighter planes, modifying them to win the 1947 and 1949 races.

"Those Corsairs were big fighting planes with a big radial motor, and Cleland cut the wings back to make them go faster," Crawford said. "He was very popular because he was a local boy."

Cleland broke his own Thompson speed record in 1949 by averaging 397.071 miles per hour, but his victory was overshadowed by tragedy. On his second lap in pursuit of Cleland, Bill Odom's green Mustang banked too sharply around the second pylon, cut inside the course, flipped upside down and crashed into a Berea home, killing a young mother and her baby son.

Although it was the first time anyone other than a participant was killed in a race, the homeowners in the booming residential areas surrounding the airport wanted to shut down the air show.

"Bill Odom's crash had no effect on having or not having the races," Crawford said. "He was a transport pilot, a straight line flier, and shouldn't have been up there, especially in that little plane. After that we tried to be more careful who got in, but the races stopped because the Air Force withdrew from them."

Odom's death marked the end of closed-course racing, and Defense Department budget cuts halted military participation in future shows. After 20 years of thrills and spills, the National Air Races seemed doomed to the same fate as the horse and buggy.

However, the opening of Burke Lakefront Airport in 1947 provided a site well-removed from residential areas. The advent of Formula One racing planes provided a new possibility for closed-course races.

"A local Formula One flier came to me in 1965 and showed me films of other races," recalled Noel Painchaud, Cleveland's Port Director under Mayor Ralph Locher. "He convinced me we could put pylons in Lake Erie."

Painchaud took the idea to George Steinbrenner, whose Group 66 collection of local business was looking for ways to give the city a shot in the arm.

"Steinbrenner put up the front money," Painchaud said, "and I put together the acts and military involvement."

Steinbrenner's group created a nonprofit corporation following Crawford's earlier example. (The same method of saving enough seed money for the following year and distributing the rest to charities is also being used by the present board of directors.) The show was a success and has become a Cleveland Labor Day tradition.

In 1979 the usual 100,000 aviation enthusiasts jammed Burke Lakefront Airport over Labor Day weekend to celebrate the 50th anniversary of the Air Races. The crowd watched the Thunderbirds, the U.S. Air Force's high speed precision flying team, Formula One plane races and expert parachuters land within a few feet of a target.

In many ways the original event still mimics its original ancestor. "It's an exposition like the World's Fair," explained Chuck Newcomb, the 50th show's director. "It's family entertainment, a stage for the aviation industry and a military recruiting tool all rolled into one."

Glen Curtis Leaving Euclid Beach, Cleveland, Ohio, for Cedar Point, Ohio, on World's Record Flight over Water.

for the frail early aircraft, but bad weather also plagued his attempt.

The initial flight from Cleveland to Sandusky was postponed for a day and the return flight was made in a steady downpour, perhaps spurned on by the $5000 prize purse waiting for him.

# VIII.
# EYEWITNESS TO HISTORY
## Frederick C. Crawford saw all of aviation's greats in action, starting with the Wright Brothers in 1910

*Frederick C. Crawford, the namesake of the Frederick C. Crawford Auto & Aviation Museum in University Circle and retired president of Thompson Products, Inc. (now a part of TRW Inc.), helped organize the city's first air show in 1929.*

*For years Crawford was director of the National Aeronautical Association (NAA), the American branch of the Federation Aeronautic Internationale which sanctioned all air records. He was involved in all the air races from 1929 until 1946, serving as vice-president and president of the Air Race Corporation. The Thompson Products trophy which he created became the most sought-after prize by the world's pilots.*

*On the eve of the air show's 50th anniversary, the 88-year-old Crawford sat in an easy chair at his Bratenahl Place apartment and reminisced about aviation history.*

*Despite a recent operation, Crawford was energetic, expansive and opinionated. His flashing eyes, framed by black-rimmed glasses revealed his love for the subject. On his table laid a copy of Soviet Strategy for Nuclear War and an open copy of Business Week magazine.*

*On his library shelf there was a picture, "Earth Rise at Pelican Camp," which depicted an astronaut walking on the moon with the earth rising in the background. The scene illustrated the huge advances made in aviation since the early days Crawford describes here.*

I became interested in aviation back in 1910 when the Harvard Aviation Club held a great meet only seven years after the Wright brothers' famous flight. All the great pioneers were there—Glenn Curtiss, the Wright brothers, all of them. I took the streetcar to watch it every day. They offered $25,000 for anyone who could fly 25 miles out to Boston's light and back without killing themselves, and Curtiss did it.

You have to remember that back in those days they made planes out of cloth and wood, anything they could get their hands on, to get up in the air.

*Frederick C. Crawford*

*Above, Crawford with 1949 Thompson Trophy winner Cook Cleland (center) and Roscoe Turner. Below, Crawford and his first wife, Audrey, flank 1946 trophy winner Alvin "Tex" Johnston.*

One day at the meet it was very windy, about 30 miles per hour headwind, and no one wanted to fly. But one of the Wright brothers went up, I forget which one, and his plane only went 40 miles per hour, so he was damned near standing still in mid-air before coming down.

By 1929 public interest in aviation had waned somewhat, so Cleveland paid the NAA the $25,000 fee to host the air show. Louis W. Greve, who was president of Cleveland Pneumatic Tool Company, was the show's first president. I was vice-president.

Airplane motors back then were auto motors just better made, so all the companies making parts jumped on the bandwagon. The committee wanted to know if we'd put up any money for a race and we agreed. The only race left for sponsorship was the "free-for-all." That appealed to me. Anyone could enter, fly like hell, and the fastest plane won. We bought a $50 tin cup which was the beginning of the Thompson trophy.

The event went over pretty good so the NAA said we could have it every year. We gave the NAA a $5,000 endowment every year to take care of the trophy and we sponsored a sculpture competition to design it.

I was dining with architect Byers Hayes, and he said, "I'd like to see a trophy with waves and rocks and cliffs, birds and sky and sun and an airplane on top, a statue that tells a story." So I told the sculptors that's what I wanted them to aim at.

Walter Sinz, a Cleveland sculptor, won the competition with a trophy that included these elements. One of the Wright brothers was on the committee to choose the winner. (That'll give you some idea of the prominence of the judges.) Originally they put a replica of the winning plane on top but it became too difficult. So we gave it up. We had a couple copies of the trophies made up to put on display around town, and today one of them is in the Smithsonian Institute in Washington.

Planes were slow back then; you could have the whole race out at the airport. Today it takes a fellow six states to turn around.

At the time of the races, Roscoe Turner (his little gold racer is in our museum) was heavily in debt. He had to borrow a plane and an engine for the race. About noon on Labor Day, the day of the races, a process server came around the hangar looking for Turner. A smart mechanic told him Turner would be back shortly and told him to go sit in Turner's plane and wait for him—but it was the wrong plane. While he was sitting there like a fool, the mechanic got a few guys to push Turner's plane out of the hangar. Turner went out and won the race plus enough money to pay off his debts.

The point is, that's the way we financed aviaition in the 1930's.

After World War II a pilot told me that he was with a dozen other pilots in Burma waiting to fly

supplies over the hump to China. When someone asked how they got interested in flying, most of them said it was from the Cleveland Air Races.

I became president of the races when Lou Greve died. From 1929 until the war we hired Cliff Henderson and his brother Phillip to run the show. He was an air enthusiast and promoter from Los Angeles and always brought a movie star here to be queen of the show.

All the great pilots would come every year. Lindbergh was a quiet man, very respectful and always a gentleman. He didn't like all the publicity he got. Amelia Earhart was very attractive, hair askew, bright-eyed, enthusiastic, pleasant. Thompson helped support her flights, and she'd bring me back stamps from other countries and bits of cloth from her planes.

And (General) Jimmy Doolittle is one of my best friends. A little fellow, you'd think he was seven feet tall from his personality and piercing eyes. One of those natural fliers who could fly a plane like a cowboy rides a horse.

Howard Hughes was usually there. And many a general during the war, like Hap Arnold, I first met when they were colonels flying in the races. Amos and Andy, the radio personalities, flew to the races in different planes. They didn't trust each other.

Harold Lloyd, the comedian, sat in my box one year and didn't wear his glasses. I was wearing dark rimmed glasses similar to his. When the kids found out Harold Lloyd was supposed to be in my box they thought I was him. I had great fun signing Lloyd's autograph.

After World War II the jets (F-80s) entered the air show. They had higher speeds and higher altitudes so we created a separate division. You couldn't put a jet up against the reciprocating engine. We showed off the B-36, the biggest plane they ever built, and had great parachute jumping and tremendous military maneuvers in the air.

But the planes began to fly too fast for the races, and since the public was air-minded, the military didn't need any more promotion. Congress automatically granted appropriations. General (Curtis) LeMay told me the military decided it would rather have little air races across the country than one big show.

The Thompson Trophy became a symbol of speed records. You'd see pictures of it in the paper going to Air Force officers every time they came out with a new plane.

The races were good for Cleveland. In the 1930s and 40s a picture map of the United States would show a car at Indianapolis, a horse in Kentucky and in Cleveland, the air races. The Thompson race was broadcast on radio all over the country.

Anything that gives the people a little pride in their city is good.

# IX.

# THE RETURN OF THE NORTH COAST

## A bold new plan to restore a once great lakefront

One warm summer night in 1978 a young couple wrestled romantically on the front seat of their car at Perkins Beach, a popular make-out spot just west of Edgewater Park. A state ranger, however, interrupted their celebration to give them a ticket for trespassing in a state park after the 10:30 p.m. closing time.

Like many other Clevelanders, the young couple was unaware that the Ohio Department of Natural Resources (ODNR), quietly and without fanfare, had begun the enormous task of restoring Cleveland's rundown twelve-mile lakefront to its former glory.

While cities such as Boston, Chicago, San Francisco and Toronto developed their waterfronts into exciting commercial enterprises, Cleveland had allowed its beautifully landscaped, well-maintained lakefront park system to deteriorate into a garbage-filled vandal's paradise.

In 1977, when the city finally realized it was financially unable to provide the huge sums of money necessary for restoration, it leased its three lakefront parks to the state of Ohio. As part of the deal, the Ohio General Assembly budgeted an initial $5 million for capital improvements at Edgewater Park (at the west end of the Shoreway), Gordon Park (at the foot of Liberty Boulevard) and Wildwood Park (at the foot of Neff Road by the mouth of Euclid Creek.) Also included was $2 million for operating and maintenance expenses as well as a commitment to provide additional funds in the future.

That summer the state began spending the seed money. "We cleaned up the beaches, repaired breakwalls, hired lifeguards, provided law enforcement and built a new roadway, parking lot, fishing pier and restroom at Gordon Park," said Robert Bacon, the park's former manager, from his office on top of the East 55th Street marina.

"In 1979 we moved the roadway and parking lot at Upper Edgewater away from the cliffs to make them more accessible," he added. "We began renovating the Edgewater Pavillion, added parking lots at Gordon Park and

---

*Edgewater Park's monument to Conrad Mizer, the father of Cleveland's public band concerts. Mizer solicited private subscriptions at the turn of the century to finance public concerts in the park. In the background is the refurbished Edgewater Pavillion, the lone remaining structure from the lakefront's golden era.*

*Lake View Park, Cleveland's first public park, was called "the most popular downtown breathing spot" after the city acquired it in 1875. It was located where City Hall and the County Courthouse stand today.*

began improvements at the East 55th and Wildwood marinas. We also did a lot of little things, like planting trees and flowers and screening off fences, to make the park more attractive."

Bacon's initial concern was to give the public a sense of security which the hard-pressed Cleveland police could not provide. In 1978 his twelve-man ranger force handed out 771 citations during its around-the-clock patrol.

"People are always asking, 'When did you take over?' " added ranger Bernie Pensock. "But it's getting better already. The ladies and older people are coming back, and families are fishing again."

The ODNR provides professional expertise in park management, and the idea of state parks near population centers was long overdue. The department has already put together ambitious plans for the future, containing everything from a lakefront bike path to islands in Lake Erie off Gordon and Edgewater Parks. But even if it succeeds beyond the wildest dreams, the state will find it difficult to recapture what Clevelanders once had but wasted away.

A mere generation ago, fishing, boating and swimming were enjoyed by thousands each summer at White City Beach, Edgewater Park and Gordon Park. Euclid Beach Park on the city's far east side was a privately owned amusement park which drew crowds from throughout northeast Ohio. Marinas and fishing piers dotted the coastline. Picnics, baseball games and band concerts cooled by lakefront breezes were a weekend ritual during Cleveland's long hot summers. It took decades of planning to produce that idyllic scene.

Erosion was already a problem for the early white settlers. In 1875, Colonel Charles Whittlesey, a local geologist who turned Cleveland's businessmen onto Upper Michigan's rich iron ore deposits, noted in *Canadian Naturalist* that the cliffs, undermined by the surf and land springs, were crashing down at such a rate that the action threatened "to remove the site of the city in a century or two."

Yet as the Ohio Canal connected Lake Erie with the Ohio River, Cleveland at the northern terminus was transformed from a sleepy little village to a booming marketplace. Its completion in the 1830s caused a bustle of activity along the Cuyahoga River's many docks and wharves. The future of Cleveland's lakefront appeared to be a long line of docks stretching eastward.

As the railroads replaced the canal packets as the prime movers of freight, the Cleveland, Painesville and Ashtabula Railroad built an east-west track along the shoreline in 1852 to move the coal and iron ore necessary for Cleveland's budding steel industry. The Union Depot passenger train station, which was opened in 1866, was also built on the lakefront, at the foot of West 9th Street. While the railroads cut off public access to the lakefront, they also began expanding it with landfill to protect the tracks from the erosive wave action.

Meanwhile, Lake Erie was established as the most productive freshwater lake in the world, netting commercial fishermen over 25 million pounds of yellow perch, northern pike, bass, pickerel, herring and whitefish annually. Not until 1863 was the lakefront even considered for recreational purposes. Cleveland was without public parks of any kind.

After ten years of discussion, the city's first tax levy (.2 mills) was finally passed by city council in 1873 to purchase Lake View Park and improve Public Square and Franklin Circle.

Lake View Park was located on the hill above the railroad tracks where City Hall and the County Courthouse now stand. To make up for this loss of park to the downtown public buildings, the city gained two other parks.

In 1889 Jacob B. Perkins, the son of a wealthy railroad tycoon, sold eighty-nine acres of his family's lakefront estate to the city for $206,000. The area became Perkins Beach and Edgewater Park. A few years later, William J. Gordon, a rich wholesale grocer and former mayor of Glenville, bequeathed the city his 112-acre lakefront estate. Gordon Park included a beach, groves, lagoons, a boat ramp along Doan Brook and an upper and lower drive.

After the turn of the century, further acreage was acquired and a public bath house, pavillion and band shell were constructed at each park. In the 1940s' landfill projects added marinas, baseball diamonds and tennis courts to both parks.

"I grew up near Edgewater Park," recalled State Representative Francine Panehal, whose West Side district includes the upper section of the park. "Most people used public transportation back then, so there was a bathhouse where you could change clothes in summer and an ice skating rink in winter. Before my time there was even a big dance hall, where my mother and father courted."

Gordon Park, White City Beach and Euclid Beach Park provided similar amusements for East Siders. Clevelanders used their beaches and the city spent funds to maintain them.

In the '40s, however, strange things began happening to Lake Erie. Unfortunately, the shallowest of the Great Lakes was the most overworked, supporting the largest and most industrialized population on its shores. Phosphates, a miracle additive for detergents and fertilizers, had the harmful side effect of increasing algae growth once it reached the lake through sewer and farm runoffs. The algae uses the oxygen needed by the fish, especially the more fragile and tasty game fish, upsetting the balance of nature.

Industrial pollution flowed unchecked into the lake from tributaries in Cleveland, Detroit, Toledo and Lorain during the World War II and postwar production booms. The pollution killed off lakefront vegetation which provided food for fish and birds as well as a partial defense against erosion.

Human sewage from the postwar population

spurt was often dumped into the lake before being adequately treated. Many of the ninety-one varieties of fish which once called Lake Erie home began to disappear under the pressures of pollution and commercial fishing.

Lakes, like people, age with time. But as phosphate levels tripled, the lake, according to some scientists, aged 15,000 years over the last fifty. Lake Erie became a symbol for America's waste of its natural resources.

As pollution chased the population away from the lakefront parks, support for Cleveland's parks in general shrank from three per cent of the general fund in 1920 to .59 per cent in 1976.

New transportation patterns also ruined access to the lakefront parks, especially Gordon. "The Shoreway killed Gordon Park," recalled Emeline Clawson, chairman of the Northeast Ohio Sierra Club's Lakefront Parks Committee.

In 1951 the eastern Shoreway, which previously circled around Gordon Park, was expanded and rerouted through the middle of William Gordon's "Liberty Row" elm trees in blantant disregard for the terms of his bequest. Gordon gave the city his estate on the condition that it maintain the park in his name, protect the shore from encroachment, maintain the drives and ponds, preserve the burial lot of the Gordon family and outlaw fences obstructing the lake view.

The highway split the park in half, leaving baseball diamonds and the Cleveland Aquarium on the south side of it and a difficult-to-reach hill on the north. The only beneficial side effect was the construction of the East 72nd Street marina and a breakwall to protect the highway from erosion. In 1967 two old lake freighters were also sunk to contain a rubbish fill which provided seven more acres of marina protection.

The lakefront's condition continued to deteriorate as fast as the city's financial situation. As DANGER—NO SWIMMING signs were posted on the beaches and Euclid Beach Park was replaced by highrise apartments for senior citizens, city council toyed with the idea of turning the lakefront over to the state.

"It almost happened in 1973," recalled State Representative Patrick Sweeney. "Council passed a resolution but Mayor (Ralph) Perk was against it. So John Gilligan, who was then governor, backed off, not wanting to make a campaign issue of it."

According to State Senator Charles Butts, who initiated a petition drive to force the issue, Governor James Rhodes was also originally against the idea.

"We collected about 40,000 signatures and gained the support of most of Cleveland's labor, business and civic groups in the process," Butts said. "I wanted to get it directly into the governor's budget rather than make it a legislative issue, so with the media's support I met directly with the governor. 'Do you want to share in the leadership of this thing or put up a fight?' I asked him. He thought about it for about ten seconds and then said, 'Let's do it.' He

*Edgewater Park's former bathhouse.*

called in Bob Teater, the director of the Ohio Department of Natural Resources, and told him, 'I want you to work with this boy. Get that state park in Cleveland.' Teater told Rhodes it wasn't the state's policy to put parks in cities, but the governor told him, 'I think we ought to do it,' and just like that the state policy was changed."

"White City Beach was included in the original agreement," explained Don Olsen, chief of the ODNR's division of recreation and planning. "But the city had already given it to the Regional Sewer District so we had to renegotiate the lease."

Ironically, the Cleveland Regional Sewer District, which will play a major role in improving the lake's water quality, has fenced off the White City Beach area.

White City Beach abuts the sewer district's Easterly treatment plant off Lake Shore Boulevard just east of Bratenahl. The Rockefeller sewer project next to the beach's fishing pier and the treatment plant expansion on landfill to the north has turned the area into a construction site.

Whether the beach will ever reopen depends on the state and sewer authority reaching a compromise. The state puts money into restoring parks only if they are given a long-term lease. The sewer board, however, is afraid it may need the beach for future expansion.

"We're looking into the possibility of joint use of the facilities," said Edwin Odeal, deputy director of the sewer district.

"If the lease provisions can be worked out we'd be interested in opening the park," added Roger Hubbell, chief of the state's office of outdoor recreational services.

The city lost another opportunity to acquire a choice lakefront site in 1971 when the U.S. Army closed down its Nike missile site adjacent to Gordon Park. Instead, the U.S. Navy Finance Center took over the thirty-five-acre site to build a hydrogen-bomb-proof computer building.

According to Navy spokesmen, there is little chance of the state acquiring the land for the park since it would mean the loss of 1,700 jobs to the Cleveland area and an $8-million investment in the building. However, the state is negotiating with the Navy to obtain seven acres the Navy leases from the city as a possible site for an administration building.

Despite setbacks at White City and the Navy Finance Center, the state has accomplished miracles on Cleveland's lakefront over the last decade. And combined with plans to develop the North Coast harbor downtown, the 21st century will give Clevelanders a lakefront the envy of other American cities.

Here's a rundown of what the state of Ohio has already accomplished and hopes to do in the near future.

**Edgewater Park:** The old wind swept baseball diamonds were replaced with picnic grounds and green space. The beach was expanded and upgraded, the breakwall reinforced and a fishing pier added.

"Edgewater Park is in pretty good shape," said Phil

Entrance to Edgewater Park, Cleveland *Sixth City*

*Above: The Muncipal 3ᶜ Dancing Pavillion at Edgewater Park, site of many summer band concerts in the past. Below: The entrance to Edgewater Park before construction of the Shoreway.*

*Above: Summer scene along Doan's Brook in Gordon Park before construction of the Shoreway. Below: Former Public Bathhouse at Gordon Park.*

*Gordon Park's beach in summers gone by. The beach no longer exists.*

Miller, a planner for the Ohio Department of Natural Resources which oversees the construction projects. "All we need is some new playground equipment."

**Gordon Park:** The U.S. Army Corps of Engineers has been dumping polluted sludge from the Cleveland harbor into an 88 acre diked island off Gordon Park for over a decade. There were plans to develop the island into recreational use once it is filled but they have been put on hold. "It'll probably be a nature area," Miller said. "Toxicity is a problem."

**East 55th Street Marina:** Its size was doubled and a bridge was built over the CEI water intake providing lake access to pedestrians and fishermen. There is no room for future expansion.

**Wildwood Park, Villa Angela and Euclid Beach:** Combining these three lakefront properties will be the state's biggest challenge over the next few years. The state acquired the property behind Villa Angela after the Cleveland Catholic Diocese closed down the all-girls high school.

Villa Angela provides a connection between Wildwood Park and Euclid Beach. Once the home of the city's most popular amusement park, most of Euclid Beach is now covered with high-rise apartment buildings. However, the state wants to expand the lakefront beach property 1,000 feet to connect with a nature preserve behind Villa Angela.

In 1986 the Army Corps of Engineers re-channeled Euclid Creek to alleviate flooding problems in Wildwood Park. The state wants to add a roadway from Lake Shore Boulevard and a bridge over Euclid Creek as part of Wildwood's renovation.

"Our goal is to provide more green space and public access to Lake Erie in a heavily populated urban area," said Miller.

**Lakefront Bike Path:** Phase I will connect Wildwood, Villa Angela and Euclid Beach by 1996. Phase II will connect Euclid Beach to the North Coast Harbor downtown. "We already have the alignment in place, " Miller said. Phase III would connect North Coast Harbor with Edgewater Park. That section is still being planned.

All of these projects together would not have brought one extra visitor to the lakefront if it had not been for a great improvement in Lake Erie's water quality.

"Twenty years ago Lake Erie was a world class example of gross pollution," explained Dr. Paul Bertram, an environmental scientist from the Federal EPA's Great Lakes National Program office in Chicago. "Today it is a world class example of reversing the pollution process."

"In the last 20 years the U.S. and Canada have spent $8 billion to reduce the lake's phosphate level," Bertram added. "This reduces algae growth which makes more oxygen for fish and insects."

Much of this improvement is due to upgrading Cleveland's three sewage plants and sewer lines.

"The Cuyahoga River has made dramatic improve-

WHITE CITY, CLEVELAND, O.

*White City Beach, once a popular amusement park, is today the site of a battle between the state park system and the regional sewer board.*

ments since 1980," said Steve Tuckerman, an Ohio EPA environmental scientist. "We've found steelhead trout entering the river from Lake Erie and travelling as far upstream as Independence. And they need clean water to survive."

As Lake Erie's water quality continues to improve so does its shoreline, especially near downtown. In 1980 Mayor Voinovich appointed a waterfront steering committee to provide lakefront access for Cleveland's small downtown residence community. It was something the city had lacked for over 100 years. The seeds they planted are set to blossom just in time for the city's bicentennial celebration in 1996.

The North Coast Harbor will include the following projects, slated to amaze both residents and visitors alike.

**The Rock and Roll Hall of Fame and Museum:** Designed by internationally acclaimed architect I.M. Pei, the 150,000 square foot temple includes a 165 foot tower, high tech displays, revolving exhibits and rock memorabilia.

**The Great Lakes Museum of Science, Environment and Technology:** One of the ten largest science centers in the country, this interactive, hands-on educa-

tional facility will make science more accessible and informative to the general public and school children alike.

**The William Mather Museum:** The 618 foot retired iron ore boat offers a glimpse of what life was like transversing Lake Erie's treacherous waters. It is already docked just east of the East Ninth Street pier.

**The Great Waters Aquarium:** The nation's first "fourth generation" aquarium will contain exhibits on Great Rivers, Great Lakes and Great Oceans, including a 200 foot long acrylic tunnel through a huge Lake Erie fish tank.

**The Whiskey Island Marina:** This development will replace a trash-filled 35 acre area just west of the Cuyahoga River's mouth with a boater's paradise, just minutes from downtown Cleveland.

"Ours should be the premier waterfront in the country," said Dave Gilbert, Director of Marketing and Development for North Coast Harbor Inc. "There will be one unified destination for passive waterfront recreation, not just visiting museums."

After decades of drought, Cleveland will once again have a lakefront it can use and enjoy.

Exterior largest and finest Dancing
Pavilion in the World,
Euclid Beach, Cleveland, Ohio.

On the Shore at Euclid Beach, Cleveland, Ohio.

*Above: Exterior of the largest dancing pavilion in the world in the early 20th century at Euclid Beach Amusement Park. Below: Bathers at Euclid Beach's beach during the park's heyday. The state of Ohio plans to restore and expand the beach.*

*Above: The spectacular Rock and Roll Hall of Fame and Museum, designed by internationally acclaimed architect I.M. Pei, will anchor Cleveland's North Coast Harbor complex. Below: The Great Lakes Museum of Science, Environment and Technology is a four story structure overlooking Lake Erie just across the North Coast basin from the Rock Hall.*

*Above: The North Coast Harbor complex will surround the basin just east of Cleveland Stadium giving the city's lakefront a whole new look for the 21st century. Below: The Great Waters Aquarium will include a 200 foot long underwater, acrylic tunnel. It will be located just west of the Stadium on the mouth of the Cuyahoga River.*

# X.
# REMEMBERING ED BANG
## The dean of the nation's sportswriters left some big shoes to fill

It was one of those parties for Ed Bang that Cleveland always enjoyed so much. On April 28, 1955 more than 800 of his Runyonesque friends overflowed the Grand Ballroom of the Statler Hotel to celebrate the 75th birthday of the dean of the nation's sportswriters. Another 1,000 or so telegrams, including one from President Eisenhower, poured in from across the country. He was showered with gifts: a plaque from Ohio Governor Frank Lausche, a portrait from the sandlot baseball kids and, from his Round Table lunch club cronies, a trip to Europe *and* a journalism scholarship fund in his name.

The last was a present that rivaled Ed Bang's own golden heart. He immediately contributed his European vacation to swell the fund to over $15,000.

I.S. "Nig" Rose, Bang's compatriot and fund treasurer, turned the fund's selection process over to the Cleveland Board of Education where Verda Evans and Mary McDowell screened applicants from Cuyahoga County newspaper staffers who graduated in the top third of their class. The winners were selected by Nig Rose and the sports editors of Cleveland's newspapers.

The following year Bay Village High's David Nemec used the first $500-a-year prize to study journalism at Ohio State. For the next 19 years two students a year received awards which had grown to $1,200 annually.

Most of the recipients, like myself, wouldn't have been able to attend college without the program. Today they are scattered on newspaper staffs from coast to coast—including *The Cleveland Press'* Gary Pratt, *The Wall Street Journal's* Jeffrey Tannenbaum, Gene Maeroff and Ted Kopinski of *The New York Times* and Leonard Downie, the metropolitan editor of *The Washington Post.*

Ed Bang was particularly moved by the fund because college was an opportunity he never enjoyed. Born to a German-Dutch family in Sandusky on April 28, 1880, at high school he played third base, halfback, boxed middleweight, won swimming medals and delivered newspapers. Upon graduation he joined his father and four

*Ed Bang (left) and his compatriot I.S. "Nig" Rose.*

*Bang surrounded by a group of young admirers.*

*The dean of the nation's sportswriters poses with former players at an Old Timers Game. From left, Walter Mails, left-handed pitcher for the 1920 World Champion Indians, catcher Luke Sewell, Bang, former manager Roger Peckinpaugh and an unidentified player.*

brothers as printer's devils on the *Sandusky Register*.

Eight years later he took a cut in pay to write about sports for the *Cleveland News*. He arrived just as Grantland Rice was vacating his sports editor's desk for greener pastures. Bang promptly moved in and became a Cleveland institution until the News folded more than half a century later.

Always one to help out rookie reporters, he boasted an alumni equal to any university's. Louis Seltzer, Franklin "Whitey" Lewis, Gordon Cobbledick, Ed and Regis McCauley, all major figures in Cleveland's journalistic past, learned the newspaper biz at Ed Bang's school of soft knocks.

Acutely aware of the power of the press, Bang prided himself in never knocking an athlete who was down. "The man on the playing field never has a chance to come back at a writer," he warned. In a business that naturally generates enemies, he held the respect and friendship of all the great names in sports.

He wore loud, colorful shirts, outrageous ties and a canary yellow trenchcoat while the rest of America's male population was still living in black and white. His office at the *News*, where he knocked off his "Between You and Me" column in his two finger search-and-destroy method, was a revolving door of athletes, fans and promoters looking for everything from World Series tickets to a sawbuck to get through the week. Few went away empty handed.

His generosity extended to the entire city—like the time he helped arrange the trade that brought the Indians superstar Tris Speaker (and eventually the 1920 World Championship). He helped Nig Rose bring Cleveland its first professional basketball team (the Rosenblum Celtics), promoted the annual Indians-National League exhibition game to buy equipment for the sandlot leagues and staged an annual boxing benefit show to raise money for needy kids at Christmas. He also helped found an informal "Round Table" sportsmen's club which frequently met for lunch at a large round table in front of the fireplace at the Statler Grill (today Swingo's at the Statler), where they discussed the great issues of the day and planned numerous philanthropic projects.

But when Ed Bang died in 1969, one by one his many projects also died, and in December 1976 the Ed Bang Journalism Scholarship, his final legacy, closed its doors.

After Nig Rose's death in 1972, Toby Goodman, president of the Art Window Shade and Drapery Company, and Lou Kaufman, president of the Standard Apparel Company, both members of the Round Table, were faced with the impossible task of raising ever-increasing funds from a declining Round Table population. "We would have liked to continue this thing," Goodman explained, "but we couldn't get any young fellows to go out and work." They paid off the six winners still in college and turned over the remaining funds to the Cleveland Scholarship Program.

The money (over $125,000 in 20 years) will be missed, of course, but an even greater loss is the end of the Ed Bang tradition. A member of a profession fueled by ambition, he repeatedly turned down offers to follow Grantland Rice's path to national fame and fortune. "All my friends are here in Cleveland," he once explained to Round Table comrade Judge Frank Merrick, "and they're more important to me than money."

# PHOTO CREDITS

CLEVELAND: MAKING OF A CITY

Rodin's *The Thinker* courtesy of Will Richmond.

Moses Cleaveland, 1874 Public Square, The Spirit of 76, President William McKinley with Mark Hanna, Mayor Tom Johnson group and Jesse Owens courtesy of the Western Reserve Historical Society.

The Cleveland Grays on Public Square, ore boats on the Cuyahoga, John D. Rockefeller and Carl Stokes courtesy of the Cleveland Public Library Picture Collection.

The Action Comics Superman cover courtesy of DC Comics. "Action Comics is a trademark of DC Comics Inc.; illustration copyright © 1938 Detective Comics Inc., copyright renewed © 1965 National Periodical Publications Inc."

The creators of Superman compliments of Ulvis Alberts.

Stadium and arena pictures compliments of Gateway Development Corporation.

RainForest picture compliments of Metroparks Zoo.

Tower City photo compliments of Tower City Center.

WHEN EUCLID AVENUE WAS SOMEBODY

Trees, homes of Williamson, Everett, Brush, Stone, Johnson, and Brush windmill courtesy of the Western Reserve Historical Society.

Homes of Rockefeller and Winslow and "Sleigh Racing on Euclid Avenue" painting by Joseph Egan courtesy of the Cleveland Public Library Picture Collection.

THE TERMINAL TOWER

The Terminal Tower complex, O.P. Van Sweringen and first construction picture courtesy of the Western Reserve Historical Society.

M.J. Van Sweringen, proposed Mall railroad station, early plans for the terminal and train concourse postcards courtesy of Cleveland Public Library Picture Collection.

Second construction picture courtesy of *Cleveland Magazine*.

Construction worker picture courtesy of Terminal Management Inc.

Night picture postcard courtesy of Ann Sugerman.

ELIOT NESS

Ness standing alone courtesy of Cleveland Public Library Picture Collection.

Harvard Club Raid, Evaline Ness and Betty Ness compliments of the *Cleveland Press*.

Eliot Ness for Mayor sign courtesy of Hastings-Willinger and Associates.

All other Ness photos courtesy of Western Reserve Historical Society.

CLEVELAND'S BLACK EDISON

Photos courtesy of Cosmo Morgan.

LEAGUE PARK

Cy Young, Napoleon Lajoie, the 1920 Cleveland Indians and Bob Feller courtesy of the Ohio Baseball Hall of Fame and Museum.

The 1869 Forest City's and Tris Speaker courtesy of the Western Reserve Historical Society.

League Park postcard compliments of Bob Gill.

The 1946 Cleveland Buckeyes compliments of Alonzo Boone.

THE RETURN OF THE NORTH COAST

Conrad Mizer monument by Peter Jedick.

All postcards compliments of Ann Sugerman.

Rock and Roll Hall of Fame photo compliments of Rock and Roll Hall of Fame and Museum.

Great Lakes Museum photo compliments of Great Lakes Museum of Science, Environment and Technology, Lucy Chen.

Cleveland Aquarium photo compliments of Great Waters Aquarium.

Cleveland Stadium photo compliments of Mort Tucker photography.

WHEN EAGLES GATHERED and
EYEWITNESS TO HISTORY

All photos courtesy of Frederick C. Crawford Auto-Aviation Museum, Western Reserve Historical Society.

REMEMBERING ED BANG

Bang with Nig Rose courtesy of Cleveland Board of Education.

Bang with Cleveland Indians and youngsters courtesy of his daughter, Betty Wank.

ADDITIONAL PHOTOS

1851 View from Ohio City courtesy of Western Reserve Historical Society.

Interior of Palace Theatre courtesy of Cleveland Public Library Picture Collection.

Tom Johnson statue on Public Square courtesy of Rebman photographers.

*Left: The Palace Theatre circa 1943.*

HE FOUND US STRIVI...
EACH HIS SELFISH PA...
HE LEFT A CIT...
WITH A CIVIC ...

# SPECIAL THANKS

To my parents, Pete and Ann,
who were always there when I needed them.